ANOTHER HAPPY ENDING

ANOTHER HAPPY ENDING

LESSONS IN LOVE, LOSS, AND FULL-CIRCLE ACCEPTANCE

Tia Shurina

Published and distributed by Soul Speak Press
Alexandria, USA

Library of Congress Control Number: 2025913773
Shurina, Tia
Another Happy Ending: Lessons in Love, Loss, and Full-Circle Acceptance

ISBN:
Paperback 978-1-958472-37-8
eBook 978-1-958472-38-5

For Patricia Mahoney Shurina & Stephen John Shurina II
This is for you mom & dad

CONTENTS

Foreword   1

Author's Note   5

Prologue   7

Larry   13

Beginnings   15

Him   19

Dad   23

All-In   31

If Only It Were That Simple   39

Demise   45

Fracturing   47

Broken   51

Repairing   61

Returning   65

Healing Is Not Linear   69

Forward, Backward, Reconnecting   85

The Loneliness of Fragile Pieces   93

Mental, Emotional Meet Physical   105

Mending, Bending, Rounding, and Re-Rounding   117

Marie   121

Mom   133

Somehow, Someway   149

Epilogue: Somewhere Over the Rainbow   153

Favorites   155

Acknowledgments   159

Foreword

Tia Shurina takes her audience on her vivid and powerful journey of self-discovery, self-growth, and healing. Through raw vulnerability, she courageously allows us to enter her inner world and past experiences to show us her journey in understanding the complexity of self, others, and the intertwined experiences. Even if readers don't necessarily relate to every specific topic, most will likely connect with the core themes, which speak to emotions and experiences that are widely felt and deeply human.

Using emotionally resonant language and through unveiling memories, she brings both her joyful and painful experiences to life, illuminating the path they paved toward deep, transformative insights about herself and the human experience. By reflecting on her own healing journey and the insights she's gained along the way, she offers more than just an autobiography—she becomes a living example and guidance of what's possible.

She invites her audience to walk alongside her as she navigates each traumatic experience with grace, emerging stronger and more resilient each time. With an open heart, she breaks the cycle of intergenerational trauma, proving that healing is not only possible but transformative.

Connections and support are key elements ingrained into her writing—the importance of having someone to turn to—whether a professional, a trusted confidant, or the divine—who can offer love and support during times of need. She speaks to a universal truth: We are not meant to walk through life alone. From a spiritual perspective, she emphasizes that building healing connections not only nurtures our well-being but also strengthens our spiritual bonds, reminding us that we are all interconnected under the universe.

She not only highlights the courage and significance of reaching out for support, she also personifies the strength it takes to ask for it, the transformative power of mutual support, and the profound healing that comes through vulnerability and authentic connection—with oneself, with others, and with something greater.

The majority of us carry some relational wounds rooted in early caregivers or formative life experiences. As we move through life, relationships—whether brief or long-lasting—can stir up old pain, feel overwhelming, and yet, profoundly heal us. With the right support and internal resources, these experiences can become mirrors that help us explore our internal reality, process these unresolved wounds, and move toward deeper self-understanding.

Over time, this journey nurtures a deeper sense of connection—both within ourselves and with others—opening the door to a more authentic way of living. From that grounded and aligned place, we're able to face life's challenges with greater patience, compassion, and love, and begin to remember the wholeness that's always been within us. It is from here that we can truly thrive—expressing our full selves, trusting we are exactly where we need to be, and believing that the best is still unfolding.

Tia beautifully embodies this truth, and boldly demonstrates it throughout her path of resiliency. Her book offers a powerful reminder and inspiration to others that they, too, are capable of enlightenment and healing. A true gift to the world.

Yuliya Leonova
Mental Health Clinician

Author's Note

I don't know with *any* certainty *any* of the answers to *any* of my questions with regards to *any* of *his* decisions or *any* of the reasons behind *any* of his choices. That's his truth to tell—his story to share, his answers to give, if he ever chooses to. I can only share how my private words and wish to help him heal some fatherly wounds affected me as I stayed devoted, even as many of my own childhood wounds opened wide after I was told none of what was shared in a book I was about to publish for him, for *us,* had ever happened. I can only share how *this* time the girl was gonna stay, just like B. J. Thomas and I assured him I would when we sang it to him, and how *his* leaving, long before I ever even knew he was gone, affected me after a forgotten poem morphed me into a forgettable person who almost transformed into nonexistence, as my entire life felt more and more erased. I share only *my* certainties, *my* sureties (and un-sureties), and insecurities too, *my* truths. He'd told me privately he'd move through a torrential downpour to make it to me in one of his fantastically romantic love letters. And I would not disbelieve him, even as I began doubting my

God. I can share only what was going on within *my* own heart as I held tight to his hand after my promise and prayer to both. I can only share what was going on in *my* own mind, *my* own self, even though I felt so sure by then *we* shared a soul after I'd given him mine to use as his own. *My* choices, ones he never made me think, feel, do, or write anything about. As I write about it now, I sing Lauren Daigle's "Rescue" to myself after singing it to him for a long time even though I already knew . . . you can't save another . . . we can only save ourselves. Of course we can help, but ultimately, our lives rest in our own holy hands. And as I share, I want to be clear . . . I speak only for myself. These are *my* thoughts. *My* feelings. This is *my* love song of a lifetime.

Prologue

Stay close to anything that makes you glad you are alive.
—Ḥāfez

After more than half a life with a good man I loved very much but realized early on that something was missing with Larry, when I finally knew what it was, then allowed it to touch me, the yearn to hold onto it overtook me in the most fantastical way. And I went All-In for it after I was given the opportunity, the chance, the choice, the gift, to do just that. And as I stayed All-In, I kept faith I was not alone.

My favorite TV channel is Music Choice: Soundscapes, where inspirational quotes accompany the instrumental melodies. It's there the Dalai Lama was quoted, sharing his belief that the ultimate source of our own happiness is our mental state. My mental state traveled far back after the last chapter of my first book closed, to before the time my faith, and my God, became my *soul* support. And while I still trust the heavens above are our truest North Star, I've come to understand that a talk with a trained mental health professional can also give guidance, gifting us dreamers a bit of balance in an ofttimes out-of-sync earth where thoughts do indeed become things. It's been a crazy magic carpet ride—to be able to embrace my mentality with the help of my spirituality, if that makes any sense. Making peace with my truth, as I finally did with the ending of my marriage, held an important key for me, even if I had to fear losing my mind to find my soul again. Napoleon's words displaying one day as a song played also helped me face some challenging truths I had pushed away from: "Nothing is more difficult and therefore more precious than to decide." I know the difficulty and the preciousness of choice well again by this point. And I know when our ability to decide is compromised; difficult situations can seem almost insurmountable. I'm thankful for the assistance to turn down the volume on the negative self-talk that was affecting my ability to make my decisions, so I could keep the other voices where they belong—in front of my heart, not behind it. I'm appreciative of all the assistance, all the angels and guides and friends on the other side with my father at the forefront of them all at this point, that returned me to a place that feels a healthy balance as I make my way in a world where our human brains may separate us, but Glenda Green, an artist and secular painter whose life and world would take a turn toward the spiritual when she was asked to paint a portrait of Jesus Christ, assures me in the pages of her book *Love Without End*, our hearts and souls connect us, and that love never ends.

I'd like to begin this second book, and trip backward, with the ending days of June, just before the Fourth of July weekend 2015 and a few weeks before *Everything and a Happy Ending*'s publishing date. One that started with a trip to a hospital emergency room rather than my bungalow at the beach, which is where I always spent the Fourth of July.

I woke up one morning at the end of June with a headache I couldn't alleviate. While it hurt, it wasn't as strong as the migraines that could shut me down. I was so grateful these debilitating headaches weren't making a reentrance at this important time of my life that I actually chastised myself for wincing when the pain woke me from the little sleep I was able to get. A small, intimate gathering to honor the book's birthday was scheduled for the end of July. I had picked my father's favorite number for the date: 7/29 for his firehouse in the South Bronx, Ladder 29—a small but heartfelt gesture to the man who'd given me the gift of old *and* new life. Every detail of the evening was to be tended to with sentimentality, including the tarot card reader who was hired to offer guests the gift if they were interested. I've long loved the deck's symbolization of the life cycle . . . The Fool, the first card, leaping off into the unknowingness after birth, and The World, the last card, ending the cycle, ready to start again. I began using it many years ago, eventually becoming one of the most revered supports in my toolbox as I made my way. I was a mess, though, between managing so much confusion, overwhelming fear, and a most specific pain related to the book's release. I understood the root of my fear. But I was *in love*, and that was a way bigger deal to me. And I chose not to fight it or push against it, but accept it.

I remained reminded of all that as I typed, as I was each and every time I started to quake in my boots again, the shake I shared privately as well as referenced publicly, when the fear of intimacy would now include sharing not just with him privately, nor even semi-privately, but with *his* very public world. And I remembered again the faith that became my new North Star—the trust that told me it was important

I face those fears as I helped him face his so *we* could finally face each other.

But my trust, by now, had delivered me to a place where a painful ache in the back of my head turned intense. It was so bad it pushed me to believe an aneurysm might be about to burst, and I broke down. A complete and total collapse that curled me into a ball on my bed. When I told my sister I couldn't go to the beach that holiday weekend because of the pain, she refused to go without me unless I met her at her hospital. I would never have gone on my own, but an old comfort zone, one that told me I was the reason for ruining everyone else's anything, weighed heavily on me, and I relented. I'm grateful to this day that she insisted. As much as I'd been trying to leave that comfort zone behind (forever it seemed) and unbeknownst to my body of pain at that time, but buried somewhere within, was my truth. I knew it was in my best interest to go that day, which I feel is truly why I did wind up in that emergency room, no matter what my brain and pain told me was the real reason I *should* go. On that summer morning, though, my head seemed to know better, and certainly spoke louder, than what my heart and soul's deep inner knowing knew well. That intuition would be talked over and almost disappear completely by one fall morning four years later.

The doctor who read my MRI wasn't surprised by my pain—all four of my sinuses were almost 100 percent blocked. I went home with some strong pain meds and a prescription for a powerful antibiotic. My sister went to the bungalow, thankfully, after the doctor assured her I was safe. I rested a bit easier, but even with the good doctor's diagnosis I decided I needed to write a letter to my sons, Sam and Mac, just in case. *What if he made a mistake? What if the MRI was wrong? What if someone, somehow, someway missed something and I was about to die?*

It'd crossed my mind, and heart, more than once in the few years that had preceded this event, *maybe it was my time.* Maybe it was not meant to be, no matter what the doctor said *should* be. What if the book was my legacy, and God was giving me the opportunity *to go home* now? What if my higher self was ready? *What if?* After their letters were written, but before they would get added to the special boxes I began when they were born, I settled into the covers for some long overdue sleep. When I awoke a few hours later, I googled "sinus issues." I searched sites dedicated to the Eastern, and the Western, as well as the Return; to any philosophy, faith, or science that might shed some light on my affliction so I could help heal it. I was a migraine sufferer with a kneecap that popped out of socket painfully and regularly as a young girl; a teen who lost her voice from frequent bouts of laryngitis that continued into womanhood, even after a doctor eventually took my tonsils out in my twenties, assuring me it would stop the infections that kept causing my inability to speak—it didn't. That was, is, *my* chronic health stuff. I'd never had a sinus infection before, as far as I knew. I didn't know much about them. As I read "repressed anger, irritation, and frustration, usually with one significant person in your life, for feeling invalidated, for having to stuff down emotions that are trying to surface," I was not surprised, even if it distressed me. It made so much sense, as it felt so right; so aligned with what I was experiencing. I cried as I read healer and intuitive Jennifer Elizabeth Masters's notes on her blog: "When we suppress our feelings, they have to go somewhere . . . emotions are meant to move, not be immobilized . . . thoughts are formulated in the Prefrontal Cortex of the brain, immediately above the sinus cavity. It makes sense that these thoughts slide down, and ferment in the sinus cavity causing a brew that becomes painful."

I believe with all my heart what many of my spiritual teachers have taught me ... sickness in the physical human body often has deep roots in our emotional, mental, or spiritual bodies and that we have all the potential within our own bodies to heal ourselves as well. But taking that faith into my everyday life can be a challenge some days. I know sickness as well as cures can be spontaneous, even if both can also take years to build up and break down within the body. Time plays a role in our harming *and* our healing—of our hearts, yes, but in so many other areas as well. While I certainly wouldn't say spontaneous healing has happened after four years of lingering sinus issues, I trust it is a good sign there's been a significant diminishing since I started writing again. My meditation CD has reminded me many times that when we stop resisting, our physical bodies will thrive. As I stop resisting, moving instead in full faith in my God to lead again, trusting the Universe to answer when I send out an SOS again as I open my soul a second time to the world about a prayer, and an intimacy I'd fallen in love with, I return to my promise to my father to stay true to my own self. As I do, I pray another prayer, for peace ... of body, mind, and spirit.

Larry

Remember, no effort we make to attain something beautiful is ever lost.
—Helen Keller

This morning, as I sat under the red Christmas lights that hang over my desk, I pulled my card for the day. The Vow. I took a long look back and thought upon the vow I was convinced for so long I was breaking as I struggled to end my marriage to Larry, trying to accept I was "breaking my promise to him" until, thank God, the Universe helped me accept that "til death do us part" did not mean only physical death.

I had begun a romance as a young woman in the ways I was capable of, based on the role models that had surrounded me since birth; my capacity to love at that age limited to, and formed by, the relationships and experiences I grew up with. Attraction of course was there . . . for many lovely reasons, but not all of which I would one day come to understand were the most appropriate to fuel a relationship with a romantic partner, especially not one I would not long after commit myself to for life. It took a long time, a lot of pain and intense struggle inside my own self to discern the difference and then accept and come to terms with my truth: We can always choose to love, but being *in* love with another is something that cannot be created, manufactured, or forced. That kind of falling, for me, includes an X factor, a divine unknown, a sacred chemistry that is either there or not between two people. Passion, for me, for sure can be created, but that divine X factor, definitely not.

Larry and I could, and did, experience passion. But something always felt missing even amidst great sex and immense physical pleasure. If that *something* is there, it can always be rekindled. Time, attention, therapy can help if two people are committed to reconnecting with it if it gets lost under lots of stuff that life can pile on top of it. But, for me, what was never there between the two, no amount of counseling can ever create. No amount of trying can ever force it into existence. While I loved Larry very much, being in love was something I began to struggle with. Once I knew that, it was my choice what to do with that heart-wrenching truth. It took a very long time to accept it. Then, an even longer while to make peace with it—so I could find my courage to begin the journey to move in that truth in my outside world, so that a new relationship between us, even if no longer husband and wife, could be born. As I reflected on that card I felt such support remembering that intense process and transition, reviewing what those words, promises, vows, mean to me, in the real world, yes of course, but also in my very true one too, as I re-read three divine words . . . shift toward destiny.

Beginnings

Confidence is contagious. So is lack of confidence.
—Vince Lombardi

I met him when I was young, immature, more than just a little dysfunctional, and definitely not very healthy emotionally, mentally, or spiritually. My parents loved us and did their best by us, in hindsight, which is so very clear now . . . yet, as a child, that truth was sometimes hard to understand. Because of that, there was a brokenness I wasn't fully aware was there, let alone the capacity to begin to address it at that time.

I'd grown up with my four siblings and parents in our two-bedroom apartment in Queens, learning all the while that I could survive the chaos and my dad's temper if I could just "govern myself accordingly." I was paralyzed by the undercurrent of stress that threaded its way through our small space; petrified by the possible price to pay if anyone made a poor choice or wrong move, which inevitably branched out into other relationships and areas of my life outside our small apartment.

And of course, since none of us is perfect, I did make some poor choices.

As a young woman, an abortion validated my failure in the behavior department when I returned to the doctor days after the procedure in brutal pain. The examination determined that not all of the embryo had been expelled and what was left was now rotting inside me—I had to go through the entire torturous process again. I tormented myself with the guilt-ridden idea that the consequences were only beginning since I hadn't just *governed myself accordingly.*

That excruciating experience was a milestone on my journey to find my God and forge a different relationship with one who is not above me, never judges me, threatens or punishes me, or anyone for that matter, for anything, but quite the contrary, is within me, part of me, only supporting, encouraging, inspiring, guiding each of us to our highest and best good.

But that journey was only just beginning and I had so, so far to go, so many lessons to learn first.

* * *

Too young to understand how texture and touch, how things *felt*, called to me—long before I was consciously aware of my desire to honor my feelings—I inadvertently found myself a textile major at the Fashion Institute of Technology, and not long after graduating FIT, I took a job in the garment center in New York City working in a textile shop.

I would eventually walk out one day in what was an uncharacteristic move for me at the time. What wasn't uncharacteristic at that time was my father's turmoil, the one continuing to rise inside as it spilled onto everyone outside: I wasn't supposed to be living with my parents anymore, he felt that strongly and shared it often, and now, on top of that . . . I had quit my job, once again not governing myself accordingly. It didn't matter that I had a valid reason; he was still livid. And, as usual at that time, his anger seemed intent on making my mother's life as unmanageable for her as his life was for him.

But the consequences and turmoil at home couldn't keep me from leaving that job. After my boss, probably triple my age at the time, got more than just a little inappropriate, taking advantage of my naivete, I finally summoned my courage to quit. When I contacted the New York State Department of Human Rights because I couldn't afford a lawyer to make a complaint against him, knowing it was important to follow through and do so, Patricia W., my case manager, suggested I could do more. She advised me I was worth more than that, I'd been violated. I could ask for something more for myself—money that might pay for some counseling or some more time off if I felt I needed that to recover from the experience. Time to make sure I found a job I really wanted; not feel rushed into taking one because I needed to get back to work for a paycheck. I couldn't see it that way at the time though. I wasn't worth the acknowledgment of anything more even though Patricia tried to get me to accept I was. Patricia had been offering me a hand—an opportunity on my journey to find my truth, my courage; to accept more for myself and to see the beauty inside me, but I still wasn't ready yet.

The job I got after working in that fabric house was for Donald Trump, a girl Friday—assistant to his executive assistant. That job led to another, then another, in what would become many years of being an executive or personal assistant to some high level, very successful movers and shakers in NYC.

The Universe had always pushed me along, right at the perfect time, to just the perfect place and people and opportunities . . . even to that job in the garment district and employer who had sent me to a private part of the showroom for some swatches, followed me, then, as I turned around, put each of his hands on each of my cheeks and pulled my face into his and kissed me. Humiliating as that experience had been, each step on my journey was helping to fulfill my divine blueprint to finding my own strength and self-love even if I had no idea, not even an inkling at the time, that I was being divinely guided and watched over as I made my human, earthly choices.

One of those pushes, one of those assists, one of those choices . . . a part-time job after returning home from college just one semester in. It's where I intersected with *him* for the first time in the very mundane location of a bank.

That's where I met *him*. That's where she met him too.

Him

Out beyond ideas of wrongdoing and rightdoing,
there is a field. I'll meet you there.
—Rumi

There were so many times I said to myself while waiting for him, "I can't wait to ... with *him*," whatever it might be. Everything felt new to me after falling in love. Everything felt more beautiful.

The circle of that first year I waited for him to come to me was one of the most beautiful chapters, not just in my book, but in my life. The anticipation of doing things I'd already done many times in my life came with the most magnificent feeling I'd honestly never felt before even though I had felt some wonderful stuff while doing them the first time—the clinking of champagne glasses, watching a sunrise, curling up on a couch together just to watch who cared what with one another.

And I did stop engaging in some certain human pleasures for a while, anticipation building beautifully. But, eventually, over a long period of time, even though I'm more than comfortable being by myself, I blurred another line, which is so easy to do when real life hits hard. I became much more reclusive as I retreated further back in loneliness, less resilient as painful issues continued to be triggered, missing more get togethers with friends, turning down more invitations, avoiding opportunities to just "be" with my boys as I became more ashamed, feeling my role model status barreling backwards to a much less healthy time and place again as I literally curled up in a tiny little corner of my room waiting longer and longer for *his* reach to let me know what had happened to him . . .

There wasn't really too much between us in those early days at The Williamsburgh Savings Bank. I was still a teen at barely nineteen years old, and one with a broken heart and fairly busted family at the time, which had brought me home from SUNY Cortland, when we met. I landed at the bank because the Universe was guiding me even then when my friend Kellie got me a part-time job there. We were young and both just starting adult lives, our minds busy trying to get by as we figured out what the future could be. There was a bit of flirtation on his part, which flew over my head at the time—he even wrote me a poem where he told me I was more beautiful than Brooke Shields . . . it meant more to me than he could have known at that time. And, even though it stirred something in my soul when I first received it, then moved me deeper and deeper each time I read it—ultimately affecting me so profoundly that it began my journey to feeling beautiful myself—its full significance would not be felt until many years later when he told me he'd forgotten it.

But I'm getting ahead of myself—it wasn't the right time for us then, but the Universe had our blueprints.

For *him*, though, his path was clear to the divine, even if not to him, at the time: Out of the bank and onto the stage and then the comedy clubs and, of course, then TV and the big screen. I was there all those years later at the SNL after-party to celebrate his first hosting gig, where, in a private moment as I was saying goodbye, he leaned into my hug, quietly asking me if I still had his poem.

But it wasn't time for us to round back to one another then. When the time was meant for it, in order for us to have the opportunity to carry out whatever each of our destinies were, the Universe would step in, again, one day still a bit farther in our futures.

Dad

The depth of darkness to which you can descend and still live is an exact measure of the height to which you can aspire to reach.
—Gaius Plinius Secundus

"Stand tall, Tia. I'm so proud of you" was my six-foot, six-inch father's message. His nickname was "giraffe" ... a fitting irony for a man who had always struggled to do just that ... feel proud of himself. After a waterfall of tears I was able to compose myself—this was the third time he was sending me this message since he passed.

I had broken down not long after he'd died with one of my trusted confidantes and spiritual advisors Victorya when our session began with her sharing very similar words in a message she had received from him. It was incredibly beautiful while being so painful at the same time. But also very much needed to help release the guilt I put on my own back because I hadn't gotten to his bedside before he lost consciousness. I knew the importance of proper mourning depended on me unburdening myself of that detrimental weight and this message helped.

The first time, though, the message had come from Monique, another trusted confidante and spiritual advisor. She had graciously called me in Florida on Easter Sunday, when I reached out after he had passed Holy Saturday morning, only a week before my birthday. She soothed my broken heart, even if only a bit, by assuring me the bond we forged together those last few years would grow closer than it ever was in our human lives after I made my way through my grief. She gently urged me to give myself time, and be gentle with myself until I was able to feel that shift. And even though I made my way through that grief then, I would eventually ping-pong with my ability to be patient, gentle, or kind to my own self as I made my way through the ten years that would follow when Monique would again pass me that stand-tall message from him in the fall of 2019.

*   *   *

Growing up, Christmas Eve was always a special night. My father's childhood was filled with a hurt he would take with him into parenthood, and which would wind up consequencing other parts of his adult life as well. There was a void he very much wanted filled.

As the mother he longed to pour love into him couldn't, wouldn't, didn't, a lot of stuff that was definitely not lovely slowly began to take up that space instead as he grew in years. And at times during my childhood that inner tumult could lash outward loudly, and without warning. But on Christmas Eve the inner voice that often cried out in an angst, which I had no understanding of at the time, quieted as the crackle of the WPIX channel 11 Yule log blazed from our TV screen along with the jingling of bells and holiday music that permeated the air.

He was devoted to a Slavic family tradition that honored the past, present, and future all at the same time. There was special sauerkraut fish soup he would spend the day making—yes, it was as awful as it sounds! Candlelight, kummel (a caraway seed–flavored liquor that every one of us had to at least touch to our lips. Why? I'm still not sure), Harveys Bristol Cream for the adults (with plenty of free-flowing Pepsi for the kids), honey for our foreheads for sweetness, and money under our plates for prosperity and good fortune in the new year.

We'd have ham sandwiches on the most glorious tasting onion rye bread and freshest rolls barely out of the oven from the neighborhood French bakery. After that, we would open all our presents without having to wait until Christmas morning. Cousins, aunts, and uncles would converge and cram into our small Queens apartment, and there would be much laughter, plenty of drinking and clinking of glasses, and hors d'oeuvres, which I loved.

* * *

Growing up there were times a poor choice or wrong move could seem to cause a lot of stress for my dad. I say seem because I eventually understood it wasn't any particular or specific choice of one of his children that was the root of the reaction; whether someone drank the last of the Pepsi, or forgot to flush the toilet, or needed to use the bathroom one second before my dad wanted to get in there to pee, or the choice to use that toilet in the middle of the night and possibly disturb my parents who slept in the living room. Not even to get a Bayer aspirin to help a head throbbing from a migraine, a right eye feeling gauged out. The blow-ups were because there was a lot of stuff going on with my dad at the time. Too much for him to manage. So much overburdening his insides his outsides begat great strain as well. Stuff that had begun in his own childhood brewed right into his adulthood. And we were caught in the crossfire of so much troubling him.

Sundays were particularly tense in the fall and winter seasons after he fell through a floor fighting a fire and his injuries forced him to retire from the FDNY. Those days could go either way, depending on how his football teams did. Yet sometimes, my dad could rise to the occasion. A third-grade breakdown because I could *not* get division, at least not the way my teacher was teaching it, had my dad saving the day, finding a way for it to click for me. At thirteen, a choice to jump in a car with some townies I did not know one summer night while my mom slept in our bungalow at the Jersey shore had me petrified how he would react after finding out. To my surprise, he sat me down, calmly explaining how poor a choice that could have turned out to be for me. Those important life lessons; special teachable moments, and some really lovely memories were often overshadowed, though, by an awful lot of day-to-day stresses and angsts amongst the minutiae of ordinary everydays that were filled with many moments where one of my siblings or I could trigger a very volatile response from our father.

It was best to stay as quiet and out of the way as much as possible. But staying out of the way in a small, two-bedroom apartment was not easy, nor were five young kids able to keep the noise down, much as I longed for peace and quiet. The empowering moments and positive experiences—like our Christmas Eves—were less able to stay at the forefront, much as they were cherished. Too much other stuff to push them back, and behind. But, my dad couldn't do any differently at the time. He didn't have the awareness he wound up with later in life after his own spiritual journey took him to a different place inside. And such a beautiful thing . . . when he knew better, he chose to do better. The trip he took to find the tools to deal with some of that stuff changed much for him, and eventually, me.

* * *

Communication as we all walk our lines—round our circles, wheel and deal and reel in our lives—can be so difficult. Sometimes to simply ask a question, which risks an answer, is just too scary and winds up complicating stuff that is often divinely simple. My father and I bridged a big distance between us by asking some unanswered questions at a certain point much further down our line together. That bridge was crossed by our hearts, not our legs.

Our relationship's metamorphosis began after he almost died on the operating room table during an elective heart surgery on my birthday in 2006. He was in a very fragile state, but he survived after a minor valve change came with a major complication. It was a brutal day followed by a brutal time, yet, unbeknownst at the time, one of the most beautiful birthday gifts I would ever receive: the start of a sacred sojourn together.

By the time I became convinced I was the one who was dying of a heart attack one night not too far down our road of newfound friendship we'd been babystepping on, our bond firmly rooted by then and blossoming, we would take a leap together as I broke down with him about the state of my life, sharing some very personal stuff that had felt stuck on my inside for far too long that I'm sure hurt his heart to hear. When he did pass over, finally succumbing to the ripple effects related to that surgery not too long after that fateful night, our union had become unbreakable. That choice, to connect at that later time in our lives, changed everything for us, taking our relationship to a new place as it transformed each of us simultaneously.

Creating separate stories in our own minds, while letting others determine what our stories could or couldn't be had kept us apart and away from that place of connection for too many years. I remain grateful we came together when we did, both ready, willing, and able to embrace such a bond—a best and beatific friendship; one co-created and built upon by intimacy. It nurtured the closeness that had been avoided for most of my life, as it changed our relationship before he passed. A blessed thing I'm well aware doesn't always happen—resolution between two before one heads home. And even when it does, it doesn't mean every issue disappears from the living with the dying of one of them.

The choice had to be mine after he passed—to acknowledge there were still issues to be addressed, challenges to be faced, and courage to be found if I wanted to move from healing to healed in the time I had left on this earth. Knowing our issues isn't the same as healing them. That my father and I faced some fears and as a result made some choices, vulnerably sharing our backstories, it then helped us shift our endgame, which opened a divine new door between us after he passed.

I continued on that journey without him, but I knew I had his love and support. That open door, that connection to his touch, helped me open another door. One I was petrified to walk through. My dad couldn't make my fear disappear, but he helped me find the courage to move it out of the way, again, so I could open it. So I could open. Again.

He had been a professional athlete for a time in his life, and in his core, that is who he was. His most profound advice to his young children was finally not only able to be accepted by me, but embraced wholeheartedly in my life: Hold your form. His courage to face some deep fears and dysfunctions, his devotion to changing parts of himself he was dissatisfied with, changed not just him, not just my relationship with him, but my entire future.

One of my father's favorites, George Strait, had started us on that special journey just a few years earlier when I heard the song "Ocean Front Property." I was visiting my parents in Florida and asked him a question about the lyrics. It was time. To really, truly connect. Even if I had no idea, the Universe knew. And they helped give us just what we needed that day. It was that simple. A song. A conversation. On that day. At that time. And every day that followed after in our relationship's transformation felt easy . . . one of the rare times in life when simple and easy went hand in hand. A divine meant to be, and very human choice to be, brought us together and kept us together.

All-In

In the book of my life you were the plot twist I didn't see coming.
The page I have dog-eared so that I know just where the best part is.
The one line that I will quote for all my life . . .
My favorite chapter.
—L. K. Pilgrim

One of the things my dad was able to teach me before he died, since he was a gambler, not such a good thing when I was very young but a very good thing for me as an adult, was how to go All-In. By teaching me to go All-In, he was, at the same time, teaching me to "roll the big dice" and take the huge risks that life requires to have that life well lived. My first All-In created a devastatingly magnificent minilife after my father's passing—the transformation from a heart feeling fuller than it had ever felt before with a mind blown in the beautiful exquisiteness of falling in love . . . into an emptiness it had never felt in its life and a mind boggled into a pernicious debilitating bewilderment was an excruciating transition. It was time for the Universe to merge our blueprints and bring me and *him* together, and what would unfold would be my path to going All-In for him—which eventually broke me down—and then All-In for me—which would rebuild me.

*   *   *

2009 was the year my world shifted in ways I could have never known, and of course this all started in spring, just after nature's new year awakening, the spring equinox, and around my New Year's day— my birthday. The Universe did not ask my permission or opinion as it shifted my course that year . . .

My father had died that spring and dealing with my grief, mourning for my father, had been put on a bit of a back burner nearly straightaway: My boss was diagnosed with what would be a fatal cancer only days after my dad died. Not only was I shocked with that news, but Larry and I learned, at the same time, that some serious health issues made themselves known to my husband as well. It was a season of strife that I navigated through during those days with my grief for my father, my distress for my boss's situation, and fear for my husband's health which brought immense stress and chaos to my life.

He and I reconnected during this tumultuous springtime, our paths crossing once again. Our reconnection eventually became a mirror, reflecting back to me what I had always been missing in my own marriage: a soulmate connection of the most intimate proportions. Yet, just before that mirror's magical reflection, I shared with him that I had to pull away. I wished him well, and processed through a shared moment of embarrassment. I had just before that goodbye email brought up his beautiful poem—the one he had given to me during our days at the bank and that he had reminded me about when

I saw him post-his SNL hosting—sharing with him that he had given it to me at a time when it really truly had meant the world to me. My early twenties had been filled with an inner ugliness that I struggled with and his poem had been a beautiful gift. He responded by telling me he had no recollection of ever writing it. Perhaps I should have recognized this first moment of confusion as a marker of what was to come, but in my embarrassment I attempted to ease what I immediately sensed strongly was an uncomfortable tension in his email back by making a joke about how I couldn't remember what I'd had for dinner the day before, so of course he wouldn't remember a poem from decades prior. I focused on trying to lighten the mood and the shift of energy from him that was very apparent, even though I was deep in my own pain due to his unmaking of my imprinted experience.

After that poem had been so impactful, inspiring the journey to eventually seeing myself in a completely different light, to have him tell me he didn't even remember writing it crushed me in the space I was in after my father's death. I tried to ease what felt like his discomfort by trying to convey the two-way street God was watching over way back when, that had helped us both to help each other, not just him helping me, reassuring him all was well in our very present now even if he had forgotten it. The denial of myself, the hurt and pain I was experiencing around this event, mashed with my soulful desire to accommodate him. And it would become the beginning of the magic carpet ride of a lifetime I don't think either of us saw coming that December, and the start of my All-In for *him*.

* * *

When I would run the trail at Sandy Hook, the signs posted along the path reminded me I had prayed for the courage to not just swim in those waters, on the unprotected beaches that had no lifeguard but live my life that way as well . . . unprotected. Running had become an important part of the process to and through that choice for courage and bravery.

When I returned to running as an adult after a youth spent on the track team, it was to help me physically feel healthier again. But, the effects it had on other parts of me were so profound it moved me, literally, to run more than one NYC Marathon, and many half marathons. I felt lighter in so many ways after I made my way through the miles. And, the summer *he* and I reconnected, a new trail opened near my bungalow, fueling my endorphins as I trained for the NYC marathon that November.

That marathon was a monumental marker for me that year. It was just over six months since my father's passing, a few months into my heart and soul finding its true kindred spirit even if my human head had no idea. And yes, I had made it through the painfully difficult summer of grief from loss and stress from my boss's health deterioration and prognosis and Larry's health scare until that autumn where I finally accepted our marriage was over and Larry and I separated. Our differences had held us together through a long and important marriage; our lack of similarity and soulful connection ultimately separated me from a relationship I felt I was dying in.

The NYC marathon that year was only weeks after Larry and I split. It was a tumultuous time. After he came by the apartment, unannounced, late that Friday night before I was set to run twenty-six miles a little over twenty-four hours later and took our boys away from me, promising me angrily that he would fight me for them as he stuffed their clothes in a backpack and ushered them out the door, I slept not a wink that night.

By the close of 2009 the Universe had unfurled its blueprints and shifted not just my mindset or heartspace but much of my entire life. My father having passed and the grief I still carried deep within mixed with the determination, stress, and heartache from mine and Larry's separation comingled with the soulful experience of reconnecting with *him*. This time, our connection broke my heart open and brought me to the edge of bliss.

In the fantastical love story that is ours, hindsight has helped me to see it started the moment he emailed me back after my birthday visit in Vegas just a week after my dad passed. This feeling, I didn't know what it was, only that it felt so good, even amid much fear. And I feel it was something the divine always knew, even if we didn't all those years ago when we first met at the bank. It was no accident, us finding each other, someone had a hand in it long before we ever knew. Now I knew. It seemed he did too. It was time. Time to round a new circle. Together. A holy lesson in love of a lifetime about fate and destiny, kismet and kindred spirits, synchronicity and serendipity.

Allowing my vulnerability with *him* has been one of the most beautifully visceral things I've ever done and probably the most powerful connection to my intuition. Its result, going All-In with him, was one of the most extraordinary experiences of my life. You can't have your best day ever, unless you know your worst, and I certainly know them both by now. That's the gift of the All-In experience—doesn't matter if you win or lose; it's the choice to get in the game. My Hall-of-Fame-athlete father taught me that. And after he died, I decided to play with all my heart, which was one of the most euphoric feelings I'd ever felt in my life. And *he* was instrumental in helping me choose to continue playing that way.

The Universe devoted itself to helping as well. And this love story moved along with all of us participating, each of us co-creating, always providing an appropriate assist, even using my most favorite candy, Sour Patch Kids, to remind me of the kind of woman I *don't* want to be. *Sour.* Envious. Vindictive. They all helped me, each giving me the opportunity to embrace an answer to my own question: Would I face ridicule, move through mockery, allow judgment, criticism, and unkindness from others to chip away at me for a beloved? I wanted someone who would stand in the center of the fire with me and not shrink back. But, the more beautiful question was, would I stay there myself?

Garth Brooks's music sang back up to my dad in the few years before he died as I babystepped into country music myself. My dad loved country music. He felt it captured the human condition and reflected it back in song beautifully. He especially loved the genre of *true* country. He listened to them all: Merle, Hank, Conway, Crystal, Loretta, Tammy. Johnny Cash's story touched him, as did George Strait's tragedy. He loved the genre so much Joe Diffie was referenced in his eulogy. My favorite had always been '70s music, I was never too fond of country, but as we grew closer, my dad's harmonization with the slow and aching tunes of so many of his favorites helped to mobilize the courage I needed to finally let go of the control that brought safety and security to some areas of my life, but had led me to feeling empty in other areas. Their inspiration and encouragement helped me start honoring the yearning for intimacy in my most important love relationship that was burning deep in my soul.

It's as true to me now as it was when I heard it sung at the *Love* show in Las Vegas—a tribute to The Beatles and a gift from *him* for me and my friends the day after my birthday—all you need is love. *He* gave me the love story I always wanted. The most fantastical, spectacular, purest reconnection, courting, and love story . . . a dream come true. A fairy tale come to life. If I would accept that for myself. And I not only accepted it, I ran towards it with open arms, All-In.

If Only It Were That Simple

*Your world is pointing toward an insistence on conformity
which is causing you enormous grief.*
—Esther Hicks (Abraham)

During our intimate moments, I'd shared with him how hard the trip to get to a place of awareness, acceptance, embrace of my own truest self had been for me on my journey to ending my marriage to Larry. Making the bold move to free our family from the uneasy atmosphere in our home and break away from my unfulfilled life was the most beautiful gift I ever gave my children. Wanting, choosing, then honoring that intention, to transform the relationship with them was ultimately one of the most profound inspirations to help me make the decision I did regarding ending my marriage. Of course I would wait for *him* to take that same journey.

I kept trying to convince myself that must be the reason behind the delay. Wasn't it? Our story had so many similarities yet there were obvious different ones we each had to contend with as well. But, doing right by our children, I felt, was definitely one of those common denominators. However, hearing from him, talking with him, had nothing to do with his relationship with his children or his ability to be a good dad, single or otherwise . . . I began to wonder, why wasn't I hearing from him, or allowed to communicate with him? What was going on?

*   *   *

I wouldn't accept that our relationship was wearing down. It was perfect. If it wasn't, dear God, what would I do? It had been perfect, and felt so beautiful, with no trying, no needing, no pushing or pulling or controlling or feeling responsible for or obligated to or forced to be any other way than who I really, truly was inside, in that time of private reconnection with him. It was the purest, most organic, magical experience of my life.

That flip, the process of that change back to *needing* as the dominant power, my need, his, anyone and everyone's, began somewhere after our one year anniversary date came and went with no word, then continued its comeback into a very dominant mindset every day after. And I resisted that change. I wasn't even aware that my old, habitual mindset was coming back for a good amount of time. But, somewhere deep within, it creeped back in.

Yet, after that one-year mile marker I could feel that process was beginning, the shifting away from awareness, from my truest self, back to someone who based their life on others' needs and wants before my own. My wanting to inspire him was changing into my needing to help him. And that was a long painful journey . . . the shift from feeling so desirable, so inspirational for him, encouraging him to be his best and most beautiful self, to my worrisome, angst ridden need to help him do that, and my needing help from him in return now. It is a powerful line that, when not blurred, holds enormous power for positivity and change in one's life. When you aren't propelled by the need to stop whatever destructive behavior ails you, but rather when you choose to change out of a real and true desire to do so for yourself . . . to stay sober, lose weight, leave a relationship or begin a new one, it makes a huge difference. At least for me it did, when looked at through the eyes of personal desire as opposed to "I need or must."

The unhealthy issues came for me when it changed from wanting to compliment his strengths to needing to fix his weaknesses. Similar to when things changed in my relationship with Larry. Death and endings are so difficult sometimes. That difficulty and refusal to go with the flow of life can reverse so much, and turn once beautiful unions to be honored and cherished for what they are and were, into relationships that can feel quite ugly.

* * *

One summer morning in 2017, I was brought back in time beautifully as I remembered the travel bottle of Barney's Route du Thé perfume I'd gifted to him privately years earlier. I had given it to him so he could keep it close and remember I was with him when I couldn't be with him. But that memory began a time of very ill health for me as that bittersweet scene flipped a switch barely seconds later.

I had read an interview in which the importance of communication in relationships was discussed. And, since it isn't just an important part of relationships for me—it *is* the relationship, it made for a brutal read at the time. Hindsight being everything, I now know that my All-In was not his All-In, despite the glorious love story we shared. But I didn't know that then and every day my mind began pushing harder for answers, seeking clarity in the confusion that had become our relationship because there was no communication, not directly, and I was falling into what was becoming quite a sick cycle.

Because he was—and still is—a highly sought-after performer, social media began confusing me more than I already was by the mainstream media where he would often reference our intimate conversations as a nod to me and his private promises to us. But I became convinced he started using social media in the same way; as a conduit for communication since our affair was not out in the open. The problem was—because he was not on social media himself—the one friend I felt he was using to communicate with me, turned to two, then grew. And grew some more. Trying to decipher and translate messages from multiple people who weren't *him* was beyond challenging.

I knew that what he and I created together those few years before our communication became muddled was ineffable in its beauty and was between him and I; he had a direct line to my heart and that was irreplaceable by another. The intimacy and connection was something we shared between us—our soulmate connection—and when third parties became the go between, then four, then more, all hell broke loose inside my mind trying to figure out who was saying what, when . . . and why?

I wound up so wrapped up in trying to translate messages from and about *him*, twenty-four seven, that I was in a different world most of the time, walking the streets with a mind that had gone AWOL from the day-to-day business of keeping myself alive and safe. There were some dangerous near misses and some deeply disturbing days. And the more frantically I tried to decipher certain worded messages, as well as figure out the meanings behind some of the actions of the growing number of possible people who might be trying to pass those communications, the more physically problematic it was getting because I existed more lost in my thoughts than present and planted where my feet were.

Like a hamster going round its wheel, I felt like I couldn't stop circling, but the truth was, I wouldn't get off it. I wanted to stay on because rounding that circle at times had felt like the Giant Wheel at Six Flags Great Adventure with some of the most spectacular highs I have ever felt in my life. I did not want to let go of that; in fact, I had convinced myself that if I stopped rolling along the way I was, it meant I was giving up on *him*, on being All-In. When I would hear him share something in his public world that I'd shared with him privately, which was often, it felt euphoric . . . but in a split second I could do an about face in my state of being. If I was home I would feel luckier than if I'd been hit with whatever pang had redirected me while in public.

Ferris wheels can make you feel ill though, and by now, the feeling of infirm that had sent me racing up the subway stairs to a garbage can on Lexington Avenue had escalated exponentially; my mental over-whelm now presenting relentlessly in my physical body. The feeling would come on fast, causing me to purge everything from my insides so violently, it was getting harder and harder to hide in public.

Catastrophically, after years of babystepping to a place I dared dream for myself and then actually having the courage to let those visions live out loud, I was somehow now in this cowardly, crazy, sick place. I would awake each morning, knowing it was a chance to start again with the sunrise; yesterday's transgressions belonged to the past. But the problem was, on many of those days, by nightfall, I didn't care if I woke up again. Part of me felt it would be okay to die that way—a massive heart attack while I was crouched over my toilet. Or on my bungalow's front porch after purging in my bathroom. Or maybe in a movie theater's public restroom. It would be fast, I assumed. And that brought me comfort, unless I let myself wonder what if it wasn't fast?

What if my kids found me? But those what-ifs would never wonder louder than my screams. Inner and outer. I just didn't care anymore. If my death was meant to be, then let it be. Trusting my boys would get over it way easier than if I was to find the courage, or the cowardice, depending on how one views that choice, to do something far more damaging and painful for them, to have to accept a death by suicide, I stayed alive.

Even in that desolation though, there was another part of me that wanted to live. I knew the conflict and damage that beginning each day praying for new life while wishing for death by those same nights was causing and how dangerous that clash could be. I knew how important the actions behind the words were to back up our most precious of prayers in our everyday lives. I also knew manifestation was not instantaneous, thank God, in the many cases when our hearts are in tremendous pain and our minds are in severe turmoil. But in some of my darkest moments, I just didn't care enough to worry about those manifestations catching up, long after I might change my mind about life and death.

Demise

The object of life is not to be on the side of the majority; but to escape,
finding oneself in the ranks of the insane.
—Marcus Aurelius

When your mind starts to wonder if or what or who might be playing tricks on you, it's a very debilitating energy to exist in. As I ran miles with it, the endorphins, building with each foot's pound of the pavement, were able to calm the frenetic energy that fueled my incessant mind chatter. I would often hear the band Alive 'N Kickin on my Pandora shuffle as I ran. *He* and I had listened to them back in our bank days over at Jimmy Byrne's nightclub, and every time their song "Tighter, Tighter" started now, its lyrics reminded me to hold on to him, to us, to what I kept faith was our All-In—tighter, tighter.

Feeling so squeezed from outside while pressure increased inside would consume me in a moment, followed by hours to calm myself. Running helped me remain devoted to the beauty of all I was moving through at the time. Any unpretty stuff was banished as quickly as I could in order to recommit to my heart, which I was sure by that time beat as one with *his*. But, while I could send them somewhere else, those thoughts and emotions I didn't want to address, I couldn't make them disappear. And, since they had to go somewhere, they went down, where they met up, and joined forces with everything else I had organized and placed deep down as if my inside was a warehouse I could neatly, safely store everything.

As the questions continued to mount and confusions continued to bombard, they begat a tumultuous sparring, moving beyond arguments, turning into knock-down, drag-out fights going on inside me. The after effects were like some I remember having with Larry when we were surviving some of our darkest combative moments. But this time, the circle I was going around in was a discussion-turned-argument-turned-rip-roaring warring with another voice, and another person, *inside my own head.*

Fracturing

Without a sense of urgency, desire loses its value.
—Jim Rohn

B
ut, as I stayed devoted to that release of control I had committed to giving up after my dad died, the line blurred more and more between the Universe and *him*. I didn't understand what was happening as it was going on. I was meditating, running, doing my yoga. I was smiling, affirming, telling myself life was good, telling myself there was so much to be grateful for, reading all my daily inspirations as well as adding new ones, yet still, something was sliding off in a different direction. What I didn't realize was happening the more my mental state was straining was the shifting from *feeling gratitude* to telling myself I should be grateful because there was much to be grateful for—two very different things.

It had taken me years to traverse my spiritual terrain to be able to discern the very thin line that can easily blur between the two; one of the most positive, impactful lessons my dad and I had made our way through those last few years together. I'm sure it was saddening him to watch me start *shoulding* and shitting on myself more and more again. The words we may speak in our outer lives can be very different from what we are feeling on our inside, and this was beginning to ring truer and truer for me; having been reaching higher and higher, I now was falling to a very low place. Again.

When the success of another makes your heart sing, your resistance is gone, and your own success soars. Oh, how happy my heart had been watching my beloved soar. I had given him a card years earlier with a quote by Patrick Overton, "When you come to the edge of all of the light you have and must take a step into the darkness of the unknown, either there will be something solid to stand on, or, you will fly." I have the very same card tacked to a beautiful silk board in my bathroom so when I begin my day, as I brush my teeth, I am reminded of a sacred trust that, yes, I can face the unknown. Yes, I can change my life. Yet somehow, someway, at some certain point, I had not only stopped seeing the words through my own eyes, I no longer recognized the person staring back at me in my mirror anymore.

With Larry, as I controlled more and more as our relationship changed, things became increasingly out of control in many ways. With *him*, the less I controlled after I gave him the lead, the less manageable my life was becoming. At one of my lowest points when I was married to Larry, I weighed 185 pounds, which was substantially more than I weighed when I gave birth to my first child. With *him*, I dropped to the lowest weight in my life, sinking to just under 115 pounds. It was a 70-pound swing on my personal pendulum, and another reminder about balance. Two opposite ends of a sacred spectrum; two different men; two different loves; two different stories. But one same pain; same sense of disconnectedness and separation, same feeling of loneliness.

Feeling denied, not to any outer person or public, but *to me* . . . feeling invisible again to my own self, is not just the heart of many of these chapters, but the soul of this entire manuscript.

When I could keep calm, I could flip it, and nothing was wrong as everything turned right again. All good again. In our twenty years, Larry and I helped each other learn about our own selves and see such goodness in life and certainly continued to in the circle we have rounded after ending our husband-wife relationship. But, we let ourselves drift back to some dangerous waters as we began bucking the currents of our lives. Despite this evolution of our relationship post-divorce, I held great fears about returning to the unhealthy aspects of our marriage. And those relationship dynamics did in fact make a comeback.

And my ten trips around the sun with *him* helped me see so many fantastical possibilities for life in matters of the heart. In my mind's mayhem, though, I forgot a most important lesson I had learned through my breast cancer scare: Even if feeling broken, I have to keep my heart healthy enough to keep it beating. If not, it doesn't matter how many daily tarot cards get pulled, how many downward-facing dogs I do, how many meditations are done, songs sung, mantras recited, mentors looked to, classes taken, or books read. They can't make a heart heal any more than they can force it to feel. I knew the importance of stopping the incessant questions, quieting my mind's thoughts, finding stillness, so the Universe could help me make my way to the answers, but, at a certain point, I just couldn't seem to do it . . . find my calm and function from a place of desire and not *need*. Eventually, I wound up needing him—a red flag I missed: Desiring him and needing him had finally flipped. And this, along with the constant muddled communication, and sometimes lack of communication, was too much.

Broken

You can't be brave if you've only had wonderful things happen to you.
—Mary Tyler Moore

As I declined, I stayed firm in my supports: running, praying, meditating, music. But those supports would feel like they were slipping away more and more. And I didn't know why at the time. Again. And any time an inkling started twinkling, I turned away from it so I wouldn't have to face it.

I was fired from a job after only a few weeks, after being asked by my new boss to keep an important secret from her very pregnant part-time assistant she was hoping would choose not to return after she gave birth. A new boss—who had absolutely no way of knowing what was going on within me at that time, nor how a simple request to keep some things between us confidentially rather than her be honest and forthright with another one of her employees was not simple at all for me, given the complicated stuff going on in my life at that time that she knew nothing about. Either I sabotaged my own self at that job, with a little help from above, knowing it would not have been the right and perfect timing for our story at that time at all, or I was really worse off mentally and emotionally than I would *accept*. Both were true.

As I moved forward in faith that the divine was continuing to give a hand though, I continued to reject any form of human therapeutic assistance. My head reminded me I was afraid to share too much about this insanely beautiful love story. The story was *almost* unbelievable. If I was going to see a therapist to help me, what would be the point of not sharing completely, totally, fully?

I kept convincing myself in these ways not to go, arguing that it would not only not help, but quite the contrary, could wind up being quite detrimental. The fear my children could be taken away if I was deemed not mentally well, ate away at me as tensions with Larry and some of my siblings escalated. I could not let anyone know what was going on. And with that choice, the war within continued.

*   *   *

A restless sleep did not greet the dawn that day. I was anxious to see my daily email from the spiritual teacher Neale Donald Walsch—an essential morning guidepost that often showed me the way—after my night fright turned to terror before sunrise.

On this day of your life Tia, I believe God wants you to know . . . that all who call on God in true faith, earnestly from the heart, will be heard, and will receive what they have asked and desired. Martin Luther said that, and he was right. Now Martin Luther is not exactly considered a spokesman for the New Age, yet this extraordinary statement echoes precisely what is said in Conversations with God and many other books of the New

Thought movement. The point: truth is truth, no matter what the source. And what many people say is "wrong" with so-called New Age thinking turns out to be the belief of the man who instigated The Reformation! Wow.

Love, your Friend, Neale

It was as if another switch flipped in the few seconds it took to read; my truth and my reality felt completely scrambled inside a head overstuffed with questions and contradictions. I scribbled a note separately to *him* and the woman I was to report to that morning at a temp job I'd accepted late the evening before. I arranged for a friend to hand deliver them both, and instead checked into Harlem Hospital Center's psychiatric unit . . . because that was where the Universe's blueprints were taking me.

For a long while prior to this epiphanic day, I had felt like I was being followed, by more than just a few people, in more than one way—not feeling a speck of privacy in any area of my life by that point meant to me in that moment, on that morning, I had actually, literally, been tailed by *him* (well, to be clear, not him per se, but someone in the circle around him that managed and protected him).

Before this morning, I started to believe they were after me because of something I had done not too long before: I had shared publicly about my own marriage . . . the trials and tribulations that begot its beauty and blessings to help *his* fans trust the beauty, the realness, the trueness of *his* marriage, just like I had come to finally accept in my own marriage. But every day after seemed to make less sense, and feel less "right," less good. And so it was by that particular morning, in that moment, I had become convinced, after my recent public tweet and breakdown to him, that they were now very angry with me and coming after me, whoever they were. I was sure of it—sure because it had happened before, being watched without my knowledge. And on that morning, I was positive it was happening again, feeling beyond a shadow of a doubt someone on his team had orchestrated the temp job that arrived in my inbox late the day before. Something inside told me to turn it down but I needed the money. I'd been temping awhile, and the way this particular assignment came in, when it came in, the words used to describe the position, at a company called, coincidentally, Imagination, ratcheted up my fears and the fervor of my own imagination, fueled by my usual paranoia to what became an out-of-control free-for-all by the time I had laid my head down for bed that night. Everything about it had felt odd and unusual; ominously foreboding. I had become convinced someone connected to him was behind it and they were about to ambush me. Do something to me. Somehow. Someway. Something nefarious. Specifics I did not know. All I did know after my mind had felt squeezed in a vice for many years was that it was going to be bad.

There were so many dynamics which lead me to my breaking point that morning, and as I walked through those sterile hospital halls seeking respite from my mental and physical strife, I realized that I had become petrified at a certain point of the possible price to pay if I made a wrong move with *him,* whatever that wrong move might be, slipping into my childhood role of governing myself accordingly in an attempt to minimize and avoid all that unpleasantness I had crammed down so deep inside. *How can anyone govern themselves accordingly if they have no idea what they are supposed to be doing?*

Now, by this point, with so many twists and turns of events, stuns, shocks, and blindsides that beyond baffled me, and a pain that had made my heart throb in agony, I was somehow back in that same childhood place again, denying myself to accommodate others. With my insides in sheer terror, feeling ripped apart, thinking that I had remained devoted to my prayer and my All-In, to *him*; that the Universe, I was sure, we were in sync with, and as I desperately tried to honor the promise to stay true to myself I had made my dad on his deathbed at the same time, I was finally beginning to see that at some point the line between *him* and my God blurred until it completely disappeared.

Finally acting on the desire to do something for myself, a realization resounded around, reverberated within, and enveloped me from every which way: This is more than a love story with *him*. Or Larry, or my dad, for that matter. It's a love story between me and my God, who lives and breathes in me, through me. The one I was fearing had abandoned me when the truth is I'd been the one who had stopped going with His flowing. Somehow, someway, I lost my connection to my own divine GPS ... the one I'd spent years looking for, learning how to listen to, strengthening my trust in. And God wanted me back.

For so long now my life had been an open book to *him*, even if it was through email, it didn't matter. The intimacy could care less where we each were. On that morning, though, when I checked myself in, I was feeling something far different than intimacy; I was feeling so much fear, chaos, separation. After some testing and psychological assessment, the doctors eventually confirmed what I'd prayed over. What in my darkest moments, I'd worried about ... the crazy wonder I had shared with him that'd been there right in the beginning of this most unique story. But before their explanatory talk the next day, I cried my way through an intense conversation from the phone in the psychiatric ward after a call had come in for me.

What? How could that be? No one knows where I am.

I was on my knees, really now, not just truly after dropping to them metaphorically in the humbling experience that was my entry into Harlem Hospital's psychiatric care. My face pressed up against a wall, holding onto a phone attached to a few-inch cord—short to prevent patients from harming themselves with it—and I couldn't understand why I wasn't talking on a more regular phone as I wailed into the receiver, trying to make sense of what my sister was telling me.

"The police showed up at the apartment looking for you. What's going on? Are you okay?" It was as if the crackle of static from the bad connection turned up a thousand fold as I tried to make sense of what she was saying. I was too distracted, too distraught, so completely undone in that moment to connect the dots. I strained past the point of snapping as Susie told me my boys and my mother were all panicked.

I screamed into the phone, shrieking at her, "How did you find me?! How did you know I was here?! What do the police want?!"

I couldn't hear her answer, that part of me that was so discombobulated from all the years of beauty, deceit, and confusion wasn't able to listen. In that mental chaos, bawling intensely to my sister, I bawled in my mind to *him: What have you done NOW? I gave you the lead. YOUR way for YOUR life. I promised I'd follow. This is where you take me?! You'd drive me crazy rather than risk ONE conversation with me? Your safety is more important than my sanity? Or was that the plan . . . just hoped I'd die in a mental institution? Your wife following me on social media, on the Ides of March no less, was that YOUR idea or HERS? Why wouldn't you just tell me to go? How could you go after my kids after I helped you change your relationship with yours? HOW COULD YOU?!*

I became hysterical at the wonder of how he could have ever allowed the most confusing cold shoulder of my life to go on for so long, and why he would ever inflict so much hurt and mayhem in my life for so long when one conversation with me would have prevented all of it. If he wasn't coming, didn't want me waiting, I would have understood. Of all people, after all that I'd shared with him about my own agonizing struggle to face my real, true feelings about my marriage, I would have understood. My mind demanded to know on that call while trying to talk and listen to my sister at the same time, who was acting on his behalf this time, directly, indirectly, or otherwise.

I kept screaming at her, "I can't hear you! What are you saying?!" But I wasn't really listening. My mind was screaming over her only wanting answers from *him*. I had been so specific in the note I wrote to him and had dropped off at the company that morning instead of showing up after accepting that job. I wanted him to know that, even though I couldn't take what was going on any longer, I was not in that self-destructive place nor state of mind I had shared with him that I had been before—that dark place that didn't want to live. In fact, it was just the opposite, realizing I wanted, I needed, to tend to my own life again after gifting everything to his for so long. I'd become convinced they'd been watching me from afar, monitoring me for years . . . but to *this* extent really blew my mind on this morning and it was as if each and every choice made after he disappeared without a word all came together and was violently strangling the life out of the most glorious gift God had ever given me with that very short telephone cord.

The police winding up at my home was another curveball; to trouble not just my boys but my mother too, felt like a blow so brutal I wouldn't be able to survive it this time. My mom had played an important part in bringing his firstborn, a daughter, to life, and the flip that was going on in my own family continued to feel completely out of this world to me. The possible reality that he was in any way involved or had condoned his people monitoring me while I waited, prayed, sent him everything God knew was needed to help him get to where he had told me he wanted to go felt sacrilegious to me. That there were other children existing apart from his own, *mine*—living with the very real ripple effects of what seemed to me to be choices to protect himself while I ran myself deeper into the ground in my commitment to him dismantled me that day. I exploded, inside and out, on that phone, on that floor, up against the wall of that psych ward as my commitment flipped from All-In to All-Out war as I really truly battled accepting his choices.

And I fought tooth and nail with my fist landing hard against the hospital wall. He was not the new man he had told me he was, that I'd trusted he was, and a struggle waged between both that truth, and the very clear reality that had surrounded me for some time. When the doctor approached me after I hung up and calmly asked if I would like to lay down and get some rest in a private room, away from the other patients who were in the waiting area, yelling, cursing, and carrying on, I apologized as I cried. "I'm so sorry for that outburst. I would love to go somewhere calmer and quieter but there are so many people out there who were there before me. I don't want them to have to wait longer because you gave me special treatment."

"Ms. Shurina, you won't be cutting the line, that's not the way it works. Please don't worry about the other patients. We have a qualified staff that will take care of them. There's no need to apologize. If you would like a private room, we can make one available for you, that's why I asked you."

I was unaware my acceptance of his kind offer meant I was agreeing to stay overnight for observation and some additional testing. I thought the paper he had me sign was for insurance purposes. I didn't argue after I made that realization though. I knew it would be pointless, and to be honest, I was okay with it. I was absolutely exhausted. Beyond any feeling of weariness I have ever felt in my life. Completely emptied and deflated.

Thankfully, the next day two doctors shared what they felt was going on. As they spoke, I stunned myself by not bursting into tears. I sat quietly as I listened to something I already knew deep down—but had grown quite desperate for an objective, expert opinion. I wasn't crazy, and they didn't feel I needed further testing. I was, however, experiencing extreme mental and emotional duress over an already overextended period of time that I had been managing, for the most part, all on my own, that had probably begun, in their professional opinion, with my father's death in 2009. Gone was the aloof, detached doctor of the day before. I now saw a gentler version helping me to accept the fact that I just needed a little help; that I'd been managing an awful lot on my own; that it's okay to ask for help. And even though I wanted to scream at the top of my lungs, "I've been begging my best friend for help but he won't answer me," I stayed quiet. I knew the doctors weren't talking about *him* as they suggested help. I wasn't out of my mind, but unfortunately that good news meant something not so good for me and my best friend. They couldn't help with that conversation they told me, but they did advise I begin talking with someone in the mental health field, immediately. My mental soundness had been stressed heavily in my relationship with *him* on the road I promised him I would follow, and my mental health, as well as my spiritual health now depended on an ear to not just hear, but listen. Shame and guilt are two very different things. Guilt is a judgment about behavior. Shame however, is a feeling about ourselves. Besides questioning and trying to twist my reality, my mind had become incessant, trying to convince me I *should* be ashamed of myself. *Again.*

The doctors knew why I'd resisted a therapist up to that point in my almost unbelievable story. They understood the sensitivities involved but encouraged me to begin as soon as possible, as a supplement to my spirituality. Even though mental health and spirituality are interlinked, they are separate, and both emotional and mental recovery supports are sometimes necessary. The stillness that helps us hear the voice of God can often be shaken by a chatter that turns to debilitating noise. The support I'd agonized over feeling had stopped helping, had actually been saving my life after way too many other voices began clamoring around in there. They needed some help, and they needed it now.

In a beautiful moment of synchronicity, Neale, one of my longest and most beloved spiritual mentors and teachers, reminded me of the same with one of his daily emails. Reading his words helped me to remember the mind and the soul work together. Pilot and co-pilot. His words were so beautiful: The mind is a magnificent tool but has limited perspective. The soul, a much wider perspective but needs the mind to make it through our physical worlds. Through that daily email, in a faithfully, fatherly way, his words encouraged me to do that which he assured me I can . . . balance both.

Repairing

You're only given a little spark of madness. You mustn't lose it.
—Robin Williams

I t's mid-October, nearing the end of 2019—a decade since *he* and I started our wondrous, but woefully destructive journey together. I'm home from the hospital and I confirm my first appointment with the psychologist who will now help loosen the hold which my obstinate thoughts do not want to budge from. The thoughts that have become a cage again in my life. It is as if I can actually hear the voice barging into my head from my shoulder: *Don't bother. You've fallen so far back in your life, you don't need to waste vital hours of your day schlepping all the way uptown to dump your stuff on another person who isn't gonna help you. Who has patients with way more important stuff than you going on in their life. Listen to me . . . we've been right about so many things these last few years. Let us take care of you. Get some sleep. Then get up and go back to the business of fixing the life you have so fucked up.*

The dialogue was that real, the conflict that clear. The contrast though, thankfully, that strong. Just like my heart, which somehow knew, even if I could only barely hear her flutterings at my other ear by now: *Don't listen, Tia. It's gonna be okay. It's gonna be better than okay. Hang on. You can do this.*

* * *

I once told *him* I'd flip burgers at McDonald's for him if I had to. It was never an issue that I would wait, or what I would do as I waited. I only asked to know if I should be waiting after our anniversary came and went without him, and my mental state began to deteriorate.

It's December now and as I run home from my job at Amazon, living so close to the warehouse that I can do that, I realize that while it isn't McDonald's, the Universe has helped me return to my prayer and promise. They had heard me. They were listening. And they helped. Even though at the time I had no idea in the dark night of my soul that I was trying to make my way through, my God was devotedly monitoring my well-being and always had my best interests at heart. And even though I may not be proud of my every moment, I am proud of my devotion to my courage to choose All-In in this second half of my life and to the father who taught me about going All-In and helped me hold tight to it and stay the course while I was white knuckling it.

As I looked for a job after the Six-Flags-Great-Adventure-roller-coaster ride he and I got on together way back when we worked at the bank and that took me on a turn to Harlem Hospital's Psychiatric Unit, I prayed for no commute to save time, enough pay to make my day-to-day expenses, a place to rest, not distract, nor interact, or feel responsible for anyone. Even if I must answer to Jeff Bezos while in his warehouse, it's still an opportunity to give my brain-fried mind a chance to unload a bit by being at a job that is very manual labor.

I think of Geraldine, who I hunt down in the warehouse whenever I hear a rap song I like and want to know the artist and realize even though I wanted to talk with as few people as possible so as to give my mind that rest in the silence and solitude, I've made a couple friends in my short time here, much as I told myself I could not manage that at the time. More chatter, more acquaintances, I feared, would inevitably turn to more if friendships formed as the small talk turned to more meaningful conversations and relationships. I honestly did not think I could handle any new stuff . . . mine, any new friend's I might make, just anyone's, if I'm being honest. Yet, I'm reminded that seeking out Geraldine is a sign I'm making progress back to myself, even if that journey is a bumpy one where I sometimes fall into old habits.

Recently, I had a session with my spiritual advisor Monique and we talked about the Neale Donald Walsch small, intimate New Year's Eve retreat I had signed up to attend. I shared with her that Neale's daily email, which had compelled me to sign up, had been the same as a message all those years ago. A message that would remind me that the choices I made that day would shape my entire year ahead. I received it for the first time the day after I shared my private prayer with *him* to give him my everything, my All-In, and now I had the same message again. My faith feels full at this synchronicity; that God is letting me know that this retreat is the perfect place to start my year as I go All-In for *me*.

Returning

You cannot but be in the right place at the right time.
—Marianne Williamson

So special, even if starting many days in sadness still, that some are beginning in a more peaceful, positive state as I pull myself together a little more, as I return to me a little more . . . and look for *him* a little less. I remember the night before I started at the warehouse. I saw an Amazon Smile post on a social media account and grew afraid it wasn't a good sign. I was feeling so uneasy, so frightened, about so much at that time. Today, barely a month later, I'm feeling differently, thank God. I flipped it, and now I see that Amazon Smile as a sign from the Universe that I'm right where I need to be, and all is actually well, not worrisome. Well, almost well, but I'm firmly on the path again. I may slip back a step some days, but now I'm taking a few steps forward each day as well. The conspiracy theories and the crazy suspicions that had so confused me feel like they're falling away, even if just a little some days. And I think of Amazon. And I smile.

* * *

It's a cold December morning and, while at the warehouse, it was as if somehow, someway, someone flipped a switch and illuminated my world through the most beautiful experience.

I was surrounded by bustling students, hustling grandparents, and a whole lot of different energies and ages in between while music blared over the warehouse speakers, yet I stood in stillness as a sanctified moment and the intensity of its clarity moved me to tears: *He* was not yet that new man he had told me he was. It was not that he wasn't wanting to be that new man, perhaps, but that he just wasn't fully there, yet, and just hadn't been able to admit that to me. In the utter sadness that infiltrated my every cell in that moment of realization, the most peaceful, serene sense filled me at the same time. As the tears moved from inside to outside, I realized I'd given him too much credit. At the same time, he'd given me too much as well. Not in a bad way but in the most beautiful of ways, because we had been wanting to see only the best in each other. Even after all my private sharings with him about my fears and insecurities, he chose to only see me as the perfect person I was in his eyes. And I'd done the same with him along our way.

In that second, as I sorted packages along the assembly line, I experienced such a whirlwind of love for my own self and for my own inner beauty. In the big picture of the Universe, to have it go down any other way would not have done our divine blueprint justice. I saw that now. I saw that he didn't do anything to me, he did it for me, with me. He helped me see my beauty all those years ago when I was just a naive, heartbroken nineteen-year-old. My real, true beauty. And he helped me to remember it as the woman I was right now, when once again, I was feeling incredibly ugly in the person I had become convinced I was. And he did it in the most beautiful of ways . . . by helping me to find it again on my own. And now, it was time for me to stay there. Again.

Somehow, it was as if I let go of so much in that moment. Someway, I knew things were going to get easier, even if I knew every challenge and obstacle wasn't immediately going to disappear. It was all going to be okay. Better than okay. Even if I knew I would worry again, feel confused again, find something to feel afraid of again, in that moment, I felt no fear, only serenity as I was facing my one truest love, me.

As I moved through this moment and the tears became overwhelming, I called over a manager to come take my spot so I could go gather myself in the bathroom. I splashed water on my face, picked my head up from the sink, and stared into my own eyes. That's when it happened: I saw her. I recognized her again.

Healing Is Not Linear

Be glad things went the way they did. You still have forever.
—Mike Dooley

I head to the airport on my way to Neale Donald Walsch's special New Year's Eve retreat. *A right and perfect way to welcome 2020*, I think. And how fortuitous it had been, receiving the invitation—one of the most wondrous winks and nods I've received in the past ten years—his email right there, smack in the middle of a monumental moment of panic and fear about the new year, and the eve that was about to end the old one. The day after the retreat invite, as I thought about my decision to attend, I received the *2020 Daily Guideposts*, an annual book filled with daily devotionals, confirming that it was a very good idea to attend indeed. My cousin Celia, who works for them, usually gifts the book to me at the start of summer when we see each other at our beach home. This year though, she decided to send it to me in my Queens apartment before the year's close. Her note: "To be able to start off the new decade with beautiful devotionals." I packed it to keep it close, as I look to the year ahead with the same hope and faith that I started my healing journey with—one flip of the switch, one split second, one blink of an eye that can change everything.

I step out of my ex's car, who had graciously offered to drive me so I could save on a taxi, and the clock reads 11:11; Luke Combs sings the same song I'd heard the day before. Both events assure me my dad may not be here with me, *but he'll always be there for me.*

I get behind a little girl wearing a pink sweatshirt covered in unicorns in the security line and my phone rings. It's a recorded message giving details of my godmother's upcoming funeral. Peggy was my first spiritual mentor; devout in her faith. She was *this* close to becoming a nun. Her relationship with *her* God enamored me as I witnessed her relationship with *him* and probably the most influential inspiration for my own godly union. She didn't have any biological offspring, but I'm honored to be one of her children. I've been beyond intrigued by death and the wonder of what happens after since I was a young girl, and after having read Elisabeth Kübler-Ross's *On Death and Dying* more than once as a young woman. I'm reminded I'm not afraid for her. My faith assures me . . . there can be no new life without death. And somehow, my prayer for Peggy helps me feel less afraid for my own self. It felt symbolic: I must die to the life I went back to, the one where I allowed fear to lead my way through a life that made me feel so incompetent inside myself and more than just a bit of a failure in many ways. It's time to return to the new life my father's death had helped birth for me. A life that may hold fear, but trusted my ability to *hold my form through,* and not let them hold me back in my life.

As I move through the security line, I follow the unicorn. When the security agent asks my name, then if I am traveling alone, I answer, "Yes!" He smiles at me and says, "Safe trip. Happy New Year."

I start to walk away but decide to double back. I lean into his ear and whisper, "I'm actually not alone. God is with me, but people might look at me funny if I share that too loudly, but I want you to know, since you asked."

He smiles, replying, "You got that right." I'm not sure what he was referring to—the funny look or God as my traveling buddy, but I smile back at him anyway.

As I make my way to the gate, I think of the security agent who was so kind all those years ago as I tried desperately to make it to my dad's side before he died. I was calmed, feeling sure my father would be flying on the wing of that plane with me. And I trust I'll be able to stay in those calm, clear moments, when I connect with him on another plane, a little longer each day. Just as they slipped away a little each day these last few years, they'll come back again. My dad died to give me a second chance. He's not physically able to communicate directly, yet he stays connected to me divinely. And as I head to this retreat, he reminds me, *Hold your form, Tia.* I love you too, I let him know.

* * *

I'm on New York time, so even though I went to bed at midnight Medford, Oregon, time, I'm up before dawn, looking for a latte to sip while I sit at my laptop waiting to check in for the retreat. Unfortunately, it is way too early for even coffee, it seems. The restaurant isn't open yet, but the front desk agent takes me back into the restaurant herself to pour a cup. A short while later, my room phone rings—the shuttle driver will take me to Black Rock Coffee down the road if I'd like; it's opening soon. I push away from my laptop and immediately accepted the kind invitation. I was already starting to spin after I let a morning email inspiration from Grace, a spiritual guide who sends a daily tarot reading, make me afraid it had been infiltrated. I remind myself that healing is not linear and that there is nothing threatening or sarcastic about Grace's words regarding her lovely Prince of Wands. *Allow your illuminating charm to influence your connections. The warmth you give will be graciously received. This is a wonderful time to tend to your relationships of all shapes and sizes.* Yet I was starting to see it that way—threatening, sarcastic. I tried to tell myself it was God speaking through her. No one else. Yet my mind didn't allow that for long before it chimed in with its own opinions as to who and what to trust after these last five years. I remember sharing in an email with *him* that I felt the Universe had helped keep us apart so we could each go off and live the lives we were meant to at that time, separately. I thought of that journey—the one I took to help my own self, yet came with so much help. And then I'm present, remembering I have to stay accepting that help may not come from who, where, how, or the way I want it. I have asked for help, and I have to stay open to it arriving in many ways, not trying to control the details. This morning, help has arrived by way of the van driver. As I got in, he looked right at me and said, "Don't worry; be happy."

As we drove, he asked why I was there, and when I answered I was attending Neale's retreat, he responded, "Oh, you want to talk to Jesus."

I replied, "Well, not really, but close enough."

He chuckled, and told me I could talk to him, for free, since his name was Jesus. I smiled as I replied to his kind attempt to humor me, "Jesus, you've no idea how much that just meant to me. Thank you so much for your words . . . and for driving me."

He reached over from the steering wheel and touched my arm as he told me it was his pleasure, then assured me he meant what he said. He encountered many people every day, people who were unhappy, who would try to take his joy even in the short ride to and from the airport, but he was firm as he shared his faith, "You can be unhappy but I won't let you touch me." Literally—he shared a passenger had recently done just that, physically touched him in an unpleasant way.

What a gift he gave me; another moment to help me make it a few more moments in a state of trust. I have no doubt that more of just that kind of help will reel me in, a hundred times a day now if need be. I'm trusting tomorrow may only need ninety-nine.

⋆ ⋆ ⋆

It's December 31. The last day of a decade that has been beautiful yet brutally difficult at the same time. An entire decade without my dad physically by my side to help after he inspired the first real leap of my life. Knowing, though, that he's always been truly with me has been a lifesaver. I crashed after I hit the ground, and I feel quite certain he wouldn't have been able to help me pick up my pieces the way I did if he'd been here on this earth with me. But, that doesn't mean some days I'm not heartbroken to not be able to feel my father's physical hand in mine, or really hear his human voice on the other end of the phone. *Take a deep breath, Tia, then take another. You can do this.* As I look out over the hotel parking lot before heading downstairs for the last day of the retreat, I offer a prayer Neale reminded me of yesterday to help release what can sometimes be the intense pressure we put on our own selves. *Dear God, thank you for helping me to accept this problem has already been solved for me, this question already answered for me, the blessings already on their way to me.*

I hold this prayer with me as the day moves into night and the hands tick toward the promises of a new decade. I wasn't sure I'd participate after Neale extended an invitation on the first day of the retreat: On the last day, after our last meal together, but before the clock struck midnight on New Year's Eve, he welcomed any guest who wanted to stand and share their New Year's resolutions with the group. Even if I didn't know if I would have the courage to share so intimately and bare my soul before a room of strangers, I did agree with his opinion that it holds great power to declare our intentions for the new year publicly, before others, as well as God. I'd not planned to engage or make any new friends those three days, but rather, keep to myself, something I was quite used to doing by that point, but I'm grateful I did not stick to that resolve.

When the moment arose, not long before the ball dropped at midnight in that intimate dining room of the pacific northwest, I took that chance and shared my resolutions with the group, who by that last day together felt no longer strangers at all.

"A big part of me didn't want to do this. But I agree with Neale— it holds significance and importance, so thank you. My dad died just months before this decade began. Not too long after he had begun helping me change a life I wasn't satisfied in. These past ten years have brought some deeply gratifying changes, but it has also been brutally difficult at times as I have felt pulled, pushed, picked, and gnawed at while making those changes. It is one of the main reasons I'm so grateful I wound up here, in this place, at this time, before I begin a new decade. One of the things he was able to teach me before he died, since he was a gambler, not such a good thing when I was very young but a very good thing for me as an adult, was how to go All-In—thank you again for your encouragement to us all to 'roll the big dice' while we're here in this life. Was perfect to hear more than once these last few days. These last few years saw me starting to push back from the table, consider folding, growing more and more afraid of so much, again. For 2020, as I start a new decade, I reconfirm to the Universe, I'm All-In. I'm still All-In. Happy New Year. Happy Decade. Happy Everything to all of us. Here's to 2020."

The buzz from my champagne brought a smile after sharing so rawly publicly with my new friends. One, a lovely man who stopped by my table just after midnight, let me know how much my New Year's resolution had moved him. One whose words would stay with me long after I returned from Oregon: "Treasure the journey, Tia. No matter what." And another, a woman whose friendship will stay forever in my heart, my "buddy," a person we were asked to hook up with on the first day of the retreat, an emotional support so to speak, to have our back and make sure each had come back at the start of each session since the discussions and topics could get quite intense at times. Before the first session started I was sitting alone, as people were milling about, introducing themselves, when my soon-to-be new friend sat beside me. She asked me just after I returned her hello. I had to take a deep breath before I could answer her so surprised at my overwhelm when she asked. *No, I don't have a buddy.* In that moment, in that flip of a switch, she became not just my buddy for a few days, but a friend for life. Funny sometimes, how the Universe brings people together. Lori, a concert pianist and music teacher, was the most right and perfect person who could have befriended me that weekend, and I'm ever grateful God hooked us up that morning. More special angels the Universe put in my place in *that* precious moment to help.

*   *   *

Of course that New-Year's-Eve-retreat buzz couldn't last forever. It's only a few weeks later and I feel scared. I'm not even out of January and overwhelmed, beyond tired and I'm barely half way through the month. Spending so many years writing, reviewing, and reliving the most destructive decade of my life has really, not just truly, exhausted me in every way possible. I'm not sure I can continue writing, healing, turning my entire life around after it's bottoming out in September—it all seems almost too much right now.

As I start to berate myself for my inadequacy at not even making it two weeks before I'm bawling in despair again, I stop. I know I need to reset . . . immediately. I have tools for this now and I know I need to take a break before the self-bashing and battering really ramp up, which will not serve me well. In fact, I am well aware my inner critic will harm me way more than anything anyone else has to say about me.

I remember Dr. G's advice to do what I need to do to stop momentum from building. It was similar to the reset suggestions a couple who attended Neale's retreat gave when trying to manage our reactions and responses to outside stimuli. And after I stop, drop, and say a prayer to help quiet my mind, I step away from my desk and decide to try a bath. As I soak I ask God to please let me know I'm on the right track and give me strength to keep putting one foot in front of the other. I know well it's the baby steps that inspire the leaps that help us make it to where we want to go. Our mind's eye vision is just that . . . from our *mind* . . . and I am responsible for what I create and allow to formulate there. It's not the same as the brain, which is there to keep us breathing. Yes, my brain is part of it, and like many I think, I use it to refer to that *thinking* part of me. And its job is to keep me alive, yes, of course, but so is my *heart's*, which also plays a role in that vision. As does the soul. I remind myself I do have control over some vitally important areas.

I relax into the water, close my eyes, let out a deep breath.

*　*　*

One morning I utilized a grounding tool my psychologist recommended to help reset myself in a moment of panic. Her role was to help my mind regain some sense of calm when facing some very un-calm stuff before it began to reel too far, and her assistance with this grounding tool has surely been a godsend.

It was challenging when we first started working together. I was overwhelmed, thinking I needed to catch her up on every detail of my life, never mind these few years, in order for her to be able to give that help, and it hindered my ability to share with her at first. I was scared of going back in time in my mind again to do that, very afraid it would backfire; petrified I couldn't take many more trips back in my life . . . for anyone, not even myself. The rollercoaster that I felt I was inching upward on would, on some dark days, still turn on a dime when I would awake and allow the worries to take me way far down not too long after I'd put my feet on the floor. The imbalance was palpable those days. On this one I chose to utilize some of the techniques while calling on my dad, which always helps me most. Then, as I walked, my foot kicked something, and when I looked down I saw a purple hand. I kept walking, but something made me turn back. I stopped the conversation, bent down and picked the piece of plastic up. I tapped it on top of the back of my hand a few times, like a gentlest hand slap suggested as a real, literal, physical example to help reset. *Stop it, Tia. Don't go there. Stop it now.* I then dried it from the puddle it had been sitting in and dropped it in my bag and forgot about it.

Until this magical morning a week later when I left the laundro-mat. I headed to Larry's car, which I had borrowed, talking again with my dad, reminding him how much I needed him to stay close. As I reached into my bag for the key fob, I felt something at my fingertips. Being an organizational neat freak, I usually know every single item in my bag, probably even exactly where it is within my bag to boot, so it was strange to feel something I didn't recognize. As I grabbed hold and started to pull it out, I realized immediately what it was. I stood there in the parking lot staring at it, flashing back to my dad's last night on earth, when I'd placed my hand on top of his at his bedside. Instead of tapping the top of my hand with it, like I had before, I placed my hand on top of the purple plastic, and in the midst of a rainy morning, was back in the hospital at that moment.

While I opened the car door, I thanked my dad for the reminder and his quick reassurance, when I looked up and realized in that second that not only was I back at the same laundromat I was the day I had my last real conversation with my dad before he died but, as had happened that same day, I had just thrown clothes in the dryer, the car had been parked in the same exact spot, and after starting the day in a spin after a family issue with a sibling had reared its ugly head again, I had sat in my car while my clothes dried as my dad talked me through the issue over the phone. And I heard him again in that moment as clearly as I had on that call that day more than ten years earlier. "Take a deep breath, Tia. Now take another." And I did. What a gift on top of a gift on top of a gift. I wondered aloud to myself, "How can I ever lose faith in a father, in a Universe, in a love so strong watching over this story?"

*   *   *

It's my annual birthday reading with Bonnie. I treasure every second of her time and insight, especially the charcoal drawing that accompanies our sessions. Bonnie is a real and true angel I met ten years ago, *coincidentally*, after my out-of-this-world love story had taken one of its first fantastical turns. I have not only added her charcoals and gifted insights into my toolbox for guidance in managing my life, I have come to hold her quite near and dear to my heart.

My own personal New Year's Day—my birthday—is actually in April. I decide I don't want to wait until then when I find out Bonnie has an opening in her schedule despite it being January; it feels like perfect timing.

We begin in the usual way, a prayer followed by a few minutes of silence, and then Bonnie's charcoals begin their work. A usual figure shows up in her drawings for me, and today is no different. It's a large face of a man in the human body, not a spirit coming through, and it comes with this feeling for Bonnie that there is something about it that is almost like stone. "There are lots of faces around him and I'm getting the sense that this is the way I am. His mouth is shut, not trying to tell you anything. Whatever he has already said, he is sticking to it—there is a deep sadness about him. *I'm sorry I can't change what needs to be changed.* I feel from the picture a strong sense from him of 'I'm on hold.'"

He has a double ear, a lower and an upper, like he is listening to two different voices. He is in a predicament, and he is trying to listen to both but feels he cannot. Even if Bonnie's words gift a bit of grace, they remind me that it was that exact frenzied confusion that took me to the hospital, not having any idea which specific what he had said that he was sticking to. I share with her that I feel this is pertaining to the man from our first reading ten years earlier, who then, the spirits conveyed, would struggle with some difficult choices he would need to make in order for us to be together.

"Oh, he didn't choose it," she interjected, interrupting my remembering.

"I know," I replied.

I spent a long time assuming the struggle referred to ending his marriage, the same thing I had struggled with, and I'm sure that was one of his challenges, but it wasn't the most important one, and not the one that had almost destroyed me, as it became clearer and clearer through the years. I could now see that if he had ever hoped to have a different kind of life—it meant accepting intimacy into the rest of that life. Disappearing the way he did had not only shocked me, it rocked me to my core, ripping me to shreds. His marital status had little to do with that tearing. His physical presence had nothing to do with it either.

Bonnie talks a bit about the other figures that show up near his head, including a woman who appeared after the others. She is distant from them all, and her face is very white. In the drawing, she is looking directly at him, very intently, and clearly not happy with him.

Another head appeared, she shares, this one in a helmet of some sort, just like my dad had showed up ten years ago. "There is a strong energy flow between the helmet head and the stone head," she says. "Helmet head is very protective of you. Another aspect of the energy tells me he is right in the face of the stone head, about to say something to him. The energy is very clear—do something or get out of here finally. Another man is above him, off to the side a bit, but looking down." She feels this man is tall and placed above because he is in a place that is above all this. "He is very saddened, because he knows there is something about you that is so warm, so giving, so beautiful, and he feels you need someone who matches that energy. Someone who can give that back to you." She shares that he is also very interested in my well-being. She brings something up about my writing via a horse that has now shown up, heading east, which represents the future. I tell her I am almost done with my second manuscript, after using the last few months to turn a mountain of scene cards I'd created into a manuscript instead. She feels the energy is saying I am riding; I am writing. The riding being my writing. Its hooves are very rhythmic, which makes me smile through the tears that'd been streaming from the moment my cell phone rang at our appointment time.

"You are trying to clarify things for yourself," she says. "Turning up the heat, so to speak, to help stuff heal. The vehicle, the horse, the writing, a rhythm that will have resonance for many, is not unfriendly at all, very much the opposite." I thank her for that.

That session with Bonnie gave me another wink and a nod from God, a reminder that there was more than just my father on the other side, that there were others there guiding and helping me on my healing journey. Bonnie's charcoal had another face show itself. A woman with a cigarette hanging out of her mouth to help identify her. A friend she felt strongly, whoever it was. A good friend on the other side now, who cares very much about me and my story. She was clear: not a family member in the traditional sense of the word, so it couldn't be my gram, who used to smoke, whom I'd been writing about. "She wants you to know she is with you. There. Aware.". . . I knew it was Suzanne.

Suzanne was my neighbor on the other side of me at the shore. She was a few years older than me, and in our teen years it was enough of a gap to distance us from getting to know one another and be able to forge the kind of friendship we did later in life. She was diagnosed with breast cancer just as our friendship was starting to blossom, and she would blessedly go into remission through part of it. While I still had a car I would pick her up when I drove to the beach. We were both morning people, so we'd sit sometimes at the shoreline, just after sunrise, enjoying our coffee. She was struggling in a few critical areas of life. She had some deep pains—certainly some regrets, like all of us. Only she knows for sure now, from where she is on the other side, if her fate and destiny aligned in this human life, and if not, how close or far apart her choices took her from the divine blueprint she came to earth with.

On one of those rides, I opened up a bit about my very private love story. She was a sage soul, with much human spirit and such personality and wit. She told it like it was—no filters—and could warm a heart quickly and shock it easily with her way with words. A very real realist, yet one deeply optimistic about the potential humanhood could hold, even if she didn't feel she had reached hers . . . yet. She was so creative, gifted in so many areas. But, some of the very normal and usuals that hold potential to hold us back from the lives we've blueprinted before we make the trip again had done just that in Suzanne's life. A few spots and stops of trouble along her way had derailed her during some pivotal times, but she was so grateful for it—life. Her joie de vivre was contagious. She touched me in some immensely positive ways while I was moving through some very negatively charged times after my dad passed. He had turned her on to vitamin D—*so important to get your sunshine, and if not, at least your vitamin D*—she told me he shared with her when he sent an article after a conversation they'd had on the beach one day. She reminded me often she felt his presence and support as she went through treatment. I got to truly know a side of Suzanne those last few years after really knowing each other our whole lives, and I'm grateful for the gift of us coming together at just the right and perfect time to be able to forge that kind of friendship. She knew I was hanging on, by a thread so many days, after making a major change in my own life, and she encouraged me to do what few do in this often difficult life—*stay true.*

I received an alert on my phone recently to *revisit this day.* I didn't think twice before tapping on it, and I went back, thanks to Google. There she was. A picture from a visit I made to her apartment while she was undergoing treatment after her cancer returned. We posed in front of a canvas print I'd given her to remind her—*she believed she could, so she did.*

I think she came through in Bonnie's charcoal to remind me of that, assure me she is near, as Train's "Calling All Angels" just popped up on my iPad. God, I love it so much when this stuff *still* happens. So much help *they* are sending me.

Not long after, a new friend from work texts me. I was drawn to Shannon when I noticed her one night after picking up an extra shift. Maybe it was her sense of style that reminded me of my own that prompted me to ask her where she got her boots from. Maybe it was her Irishness, I *shoulda* known when she shared her name, especially with her creamy complexion coupling with her charcoal hair. I was lifted, but felt a bit walloped at the same time, when she wrote to let me know she started my book and shared a bit about her own relationship with her father as she began to read about me and mine. I don't know her well, but, I do know she and her dad were not in the same place me and my dad had made it to. Her words in that text were so incredibly lovely, yet bittersweet. "Your relationship with your dad is the reason you can be loved. So happy for you!" ended her text.

I remember the relationship section of my meditation CD I'd listened to just that morning—*there is no greater significance than relationships, for without others, you could not be you.* I think back to passing on a possible modeling contract late in high school. If I'd have followed that course, I never would have wound up at SUNY Cortland for that important semester, probably off in Europe instead which is where I was told I would be sent first, so I never would have come home from college that Christmas and enrolled in another, never gotten a job at the bank, nor met *him*, or Larry for that matter, or any of the people who became part of my life as a result of that different path. And I am grateful to have returned to such an incredibly beautiful way to look at relationships, and life. Again.

Bonnie ended that session adding that she needed to share something she felt was very important. She relays that she has seen a baby's head. A birth. She doesn't feel it was an actual baby but it was right below the stone head, nonetheless. Beneath that came up a wing that makes her feel it was actually an angel. She wants me to know there is one trying to help me. Like Eros the love angel, this cherub has got good things in store for my story, no matter what has or has not not yet happened, no matter where my story takes me. She encourages me, "They want you to please remember just because certain things have happened a certain way that have hurt you, that have made you distrusting that does not mean they are going to happen that way in the future. The cherub looks very positive to me and feels very positive as well. The whole reading has a very positive energy to it. Please trust that as you head to start your birthday year."

An encouraging ending. I left the reading feeling as I always have and trust I always will: In a place of knowing that faith will never give up on me and that I can't, I won't, give up on myself. I promised my father. I promised myself.

Forward, Backward, Reconnecting

We are divine enough to ask and important enough to receive.
—Wayne Dyer

It was a dark day those ten years ago when Larry came and took our boys from me. I knew I was improving their situation by ending the marriage, freeing them from the unhealthy atmosphere between us, but I didn't understand the repercussions for them of going All-In for *him*. I'm grateful for my boys' patience and gentle thoughtfulness through this time of healing and recovery for me. I always trusted, even when they disagreed with my choices, which was often during these last few years, that they supported me. It's such an important gift I try to give them . . . the gift of free choice. It isn't always easy in relationships, especially as a parent, but giving that gift to all the loves in my life has been as much a present to me as to them, and I am so very grateful to them for that reciprocity, their generosity, and for honoring me that way.

That mid-January spiral, Sam knocked on my door and handed me a book he had just started, sharing his feeling that I would love the introduction. As I stared at the cover of Corporal Kyle Carpenter's *You Are Worth It*, I smiled. And even though I wanted to get back to my laptop and my typing after calming myself to a place where I felt a little less tired and a little less frazzled, because it's Sam, I decide to take a look.

Sam is a US Marine, like Corporal Carpenter. I am beyond proud of his choice to serve our country and I hold his thoughts and opinions in very high regard. As I read, I thank God, and my father too, for answering the prayer I'd barely finished praying while in the bathtub recentering myself. *Life is worth everything you've got.* As my downward spiral continued its tiny reversal upward, I felt a renewed wave of energy at that moment. Sam, and this author, rejuvenate me as they remind me that I have very much been living, even if I've felt more like I'm dying more of the time again than not, these last five years. I'm grateful for Sam recommending this book and mentally sent a message out to Corporal Carpenter: *Yes! "Life is worth everything we've got!" Thank you for inspiring me to not "hide your scars," and thank you for your service. And thank you, too, my sweetest son, for reminding me I am worth it.*

When I flew to San Diego after Sam got his final orders for Camp Pendleton we had a very limited amount of time together in Coronado where he was finishing up some training. Instead of the famous zoo, or a day dipping our toes in the Pacific, we decided to spend the day getting tattooed together. I got an arrow on my wrist after a bartender on Parris Island shared, while I was there for Sam's graduation from boot camp, she'd chosen it because it was the only instrument that moves forward by being pulled back and it resonated strongly at the time for me. I had already had an arrow on my mind after Kahlil Gibran's words about bows and arrows and parents and children had moved me so, so many years ago that I framed it and hung it outside my boys' rooms to remind me how important it was to me to be the best possible bow I could be for my boys.

* * *

A few weeks later in February I am gifted time with my other boy Mac. We have a beautiful talk after he comes home from campus with his laundry. We talked about the last moments of his recent hockey game, his hopes and dreams for his last year of school, and his desires for life beyond it. He promised he would think about some of the stuff I shared with him, as I promised to do the same with his words of wisdom. Late next morning, after he headed back to campus clean clothes in tow at the crack of dawn for practice, class, then a weekend away of games, I get a text that brings such a delight it lifts my spirit and energy level immediately: "We're on the bus all afternoon mom . . . text me!"

Oh, what a wonderful world indeed. A world where my children want to hear from me, want my input, value my opinion, and actually *want* to spend time with me. After feeling I was failing my boys when they were younger by not being the role model I wanted to be for them in some precious important relationships, we'd rounded a beautiful circle after I finally began to honor my wants and desires for myself more and more in my relationships and life.

Even if I felt I was disappointing them in some important ways again by this particular point, by allowing my life to stagnate, even regressing in some vital areas, my relationship with both had morphed by then from mother and child, firmly into friendship. And that circle we rounded, to *this* new world *we* were living . . . listening to each other, being there for one another . . . because we *wanted* to, was withstanding the strain and strife I'd allowed to invade my life, even if it was definitely struggling.

Then, this precious space our relationship has reached allows Mac to comfortably share a book with me, just like Sam had done so recently. *Ikigai: The Japanese Secret to a Long and Happy Life*, a book to help me remember my own reason for living, just like Mac is doing—finding his own truth about what a happy life involves. In that moment, I'm graced with an immense feeling of gratitude for the relationships I've forged with my sons and how we've baby stepped out of some pretty significant standstills. I won't let this new relationship with them move backward. I want with my boys what I wound up having with my dad, and as strongly as I can feel my father holding my own hand these days from the other side, I hold as tight to theirs on earth.

* * *

After a recent argument with Mac that was incredibly tense and in which lots of complicated history and emotions were brought up and expressed, I broke down, feeling wiped out from trying to draw from a well that has felt empty for some time now. As I move forward in my healing, I also move backward, and some days I remain petrified that my well might remain empty.

It took some time for both of us to calm down. Then, Mac shared with me something he recently read in a book Sam had given him, and it broke me down, again, but in the most uplifting way. He shared that during World War II, to a Japanese general a heroic fight meant one in which all his men would die. There were no medals for survivors—only the dead were seen as heroes. All they had to look forward to was the death of as many marines as possible before they died for their emperor. From early childhood, they'd been taught to "die with his name on their lips." But veterans knew the last word every soldier dying in battle called out was always someone else's name. The same name all soldiers throughout all of history cry out with their last breath: Mom.

I love you too, Mac.

*   *   *

That February a year before had begun with a cry. A wail actually, as the rawness of my wounds overwhelmed me, begging my God, *Still? Again? More?*

Forward. Backward. I have to remind myself that healing is not linear. And I'm so thankful to have circled to a healthier place by this February. When the charm I'd given my dad—the one he wore every day, the one he was wearing when he entered the hospital before he passed—fell off my neck during a run around the loop of Central Park, I was initially despondent. I retraced much of the run in the hopes of coming across it before the sun set, but nothing. It was a difficult few days, even though I knew I had to let it go. I reminded myself it wasn't the charm that connected me to him but the love, and as sad as I was to not have it anymore, it was a good thing to help me hold tighter to what I knew to be most important: the connection. The love. Not the physicality of anything tangible. He reminds me often.

I recently saw the movie *Overcomer*. The final scene has Hannah, an asthmatic who has joined the track team, and a daughter recently reunited with her estranged father, running the race of her life. And we, the audience, got to run it with her. She listened to him in her ear, literally, as she played a recording he made for her as he coached her through the course. When he told her, "Getting to know my daughter is one of the greatest blessings of my life," I whispered in the dark of the theater, "Me too, Dad."

About an hour before we let my dad go that day in the hospital, before telling the doctors to stop the meds that were simply keeping his heart beating when all else had stopped functioning, I remembered that as I raced out of my apartment that morning before to get to LaGuardia airport, I had grabbed my iPod and my toothbrush. I asked my siblings, and of course my mom, if anyone wanted to listen to a song with him. My iPod by that point had lots of music on it that both he and I loved, and even though unconscious, I was sure he'd hear the music on some level and be comforted. So, we each picked a song, and with one ear bud in my dad's ear and the other in one of ours, we each sat with him and shared a last song. I chose Louis Armstrong's "What a Wonderful World," a song from a CD we had made and given as favors for a surprise sixty-fifth birthday party we'd thrown for him. Fast forward to the NYC Marathon I ran a few months after he died. I had barely slept that Friday or Saturday night, before and after Larry's surprise visit came and went with our boys. I had about a mile to go and I was wiped out. I knew if I stopped running to walk even a few steps, I would not be able to start again. I was going back and forth between my earphones and listening to the crowds—I'd come to feeling annoyed at both by that point because I was so exhausted. I was literally listening for a minute or two, pulling out the earphones, going another few, putting them back in when the cheers and yelling got too much for me. I was repeating to myself that the finish line was only a few more minutes away; my mantra, *It's right there, you're almost there, keep going, don't stop.* So how powerful a moment it was then, when, as I was putting my earphones back in for the last couple of moments and while I was actually in mid-prayer, *Please, Dad, don't let me stop running,* when my iPod, which I had put on shuffle as I headed out over the Verrazzano-Narrows Bridge hours earlier, had just started a song. Yup, it was Louis Armstrong. And while it was really Louis, I know it was truly my dad, answering me, assuring me he was at my back, helping me. *Yes, it IS a wonderful world, Tia . . . keep going . . . hold your form.*

That song was a powerful reminder that his love was still there as I was still running, still struggling. And has remained with me through every hill, every turn, each and every deep breath.

The Loneliness
of Fragile Pieces

Worry drains the mind of its power, and sooner or later it injures the soul.
—Robin Sharma, *The Monk Who Sold His Ferrari*

And then there was Covid.

I was in such a fragile state, slowly mending the gaping emotional and mental wounds I had been inflicted with when the world shifted and it wasn't my paranoia telling me to be afraid, but the actual state of the world because of this unknown virus which was making its way through New York with break-neck speed . . . how could I not regress? During that month, before being diagnosed, I came across a quote by Michelle Schaper: "On my way to finding me, I found myself lost in you." It is exquisite to me, that kind of vision for a love, but since I had been made painfully aware along my way there can be a flip side to getting lost in another that hadn't felt very beautiful, even though

I was firmly en route back to myself, the coronavirus slowed my trip considerably.

I was used to being by myself much of the time by then, so one might think lockdown was easier on me than the average person, but it became harder, actually. After being diagnosed in what was the first wave of that insidious viral virus, when no one knew much of anything at all about it aside from the fact it was killing what seemed like almost everybody that had it, being physically quarantined alone took a tremendous toll on me. Every shred of intimacy with the person I most wanted to say goodbye to had been stripped away by that life and death moment. That reality pained me in a way I still am unable to find the words to convey. The devastation that welled inside me at the reality that *he* was choosing to remain out of touch on what could be my last days on this earth, while simultaneously trying to will my body to heal seemed almost impossible at times. The public service announcements encouraging us to *be there for one another* only exacerbated my agony. My broken heart, now racing again due to the virus—as fast as the tachycardia allergic reaction to the cortisone shot I had experienced years earlier as my heart strained and struggled to come to terms with my marriage—brought about an indescribable pain and fear, and worse than either, a loneliness that felt almost unbearable.

A similar wallop had overwhelmed me nine months earlier, when I received the phone call that my mammogram results were not normal and would, once again, require further testing. A few emotional weeks later, I found out all was okay, thank God, and no biopsy was needed like the last time, but it became another powerful moment of reflection. I was crushed to feel so alone again at such a scary time.

When the call came in this time, confirming the stunning Covid diagnosis, just days after the World Health Organization declared it a pandemic, that soul crushing angst came back with an unhealthy, unholy vengeance. It was the same week a cousin would die from it, and the same week another would go on a ventilator with it. It was also the same week my baby sister, a nurse in NYC, would disappear within her hospital to treat what the hell, nobody had any idea about. Amidst all this fear, I had a sacred intercession though. My father's spirit, which moved vigilantly and immediately to make sure he reminded me he was with me and would help, would breathe me through it. After I literally dropped to my knees after hanging up from the call, a bright yellow sunburst burst into my inbox only moments later, the familiar ding bringing my attention to it. As soon as I saw those emailed words I heard my dad as clear inside myself as if he were standing right beside me in my bedroom. *Take a deep breath, Tia.* One Mississippi. Two Mississippi. Three Mississippi. *Now, take another.* From there, the words "I Believe in Miracles" came into view, and I felt they had been sent just for me when they were followed with, "Believe with God all things are possible."

Claudia, the blogger who sent it, had been an inspiration at one point. To have her pop in at that precise second of panic felt very meant to be for me. She had just been starting her blog, and I had just become a new author, when our paths crossed that first time. We emailed back and forth a few times about my book, her own story, and got to know a bit about one another. I decided to sign up to receive her posts as a show of gratitude for her kindness in reaching back to me, sharing her insight and advice. Her story of transformation in middle age had moved me powerfully. Along the way, though, as I read her writings that were regularly arriving in my inbox, the feeling started turning, paining me a little more with each post as I read from the sanctuary that was my bedroom, which could easily flip into feeling more like a prison on a bad day or night as the silent days turned months turned years.

While Claudia had inspired me to begin with, the tide would eventually turn to an eventual swing far in the other direction, her posts causing me to feel disappointed in myself on a good day and downright disgusted with who I was becoming on a bad one. Over time, as the future unfolded the way it did, reading about Claudia's joy reminded me how unhappy and dissatisfied I had become with my life again. I had taken a leap of faith off the cliff, finally summoning the courage and declaring to the universe I was ready to embrace change and had not only landed on my face, it eventually felt I was being stomped on as I laid on the ground. On that terrifyingly desolate day of my Covid diagnosis, though, I was happy and grateful to make that turn in circle with her again and feel re-inspired by her post and words after she had mysteriously disappeared and stopped posting completely, coincidentally, right after I had melted down publicly with *him* on social media. Six months after her post the weekend of that breakdown had crushed my heart while my mind almost snapped in two, her first post after that breakdown lifted my soul. Again.

In my forlorn exile I dove deep into the free meditation series Oprah and Deepak Chopra offered the world during that time of viral crisis, it having landed in my inbox from my sister's friend. And it felt like a gift from God. Oprah reminded me of a journey I took long ago: that our deepest desire is to feel we matter. This was something I was desperate to feel again, I realized through this mediation, while also coming to understand that this virus was clearly connected to that deep desire somehow, and it was clearly very much a part of that process of getting back to feeling like I mattered for me, even if I was feeling petrified for my life right in that moment.

The calm cadence of Deepak's voice soothed me, which, in turn, helped me stay gentle with myself at this critical time. I can't be reminded too much or too often that hope needs to be in the *now* . . . not the past or the future, or my fears and uncertainties will consume me.

After my tumultuous decade, it wasn't lost on me that I was vulnerable to the virus that had forced people into isolation, requiring them to find other ways to stay connected to each other. I had the thought many times that it was as if I had the plague, so isolated and untouchable did I feel. And, well, the Universe had been listening, and now I had sickened myself right into that reality. Feeling shunned for so many years felt so significant and symbolic as the segregation that came with Covid spread out into the world.

I will always trust I called that virus right to me. I was in not one of the high risk categories, yet somehow I was vulnerable to it in its first violent wave to overwhelm the States. I also had not one of the high-alert symptoms commonly noted in the initial outbreak, which were only lung and breathing issues and high fever in those first few weeks. Even my heart racing and temporary loss of taste at the time were not acknowledged as related symptoms for the public during that initial stage. Soon after, as the virus was studied and monitored many more symptoms were reported and included, but at the time it was so very new. Because of that, I was initially refused the test that was being given only by health care providers at the time, so limited in stock were those tests. Only after returning a second time that same day in tears, my head feeling about to explode from the pain, did a kind doctor decide to "waste" (his word) a test on me after insisting to me there was no-way-no-how I had the virus. What I do know, though, is how grateful I was that someway, somehow he made the choice to test me. And I'm grateful to be alive, even though I didn't know if I would survive at the time, my heart racing wildly as Covid circled it, feeling like it was being ripped right from my body at the same time.

It's a struggle to commit to bed, and rest, but I'm sort of forced, as there are not really many other options with the world essentially shutting down around me. I finish a book Mac recently recommended, *The Monk Who Sold His Ferrari*, in which its protagonist, Julian Mantle, shares that to be able to transcend pain, you must first experience it. I'd been overwhelmed by it these last five years—after five before those felt almost too unbearable at times. But Julian also shares, "True life change is spontaneous," and I remember that flip of a switch from my own experience. And I cling to that today.

I make another visit to the StatCare clinic to try and put my mind at rest from all the strange things going on inside me. I was blessed to not have as severe a bout physically as the one that put my two cousins on respirators that same week, yet the fears of so many unknowns were taking a tremendous mental and emotional toll. It's been over three weeks, and still something feels very off. My heart was still racing. I went to my regular doctor not too many days earlier, who had just opened her door to see a small number of patients in person again. But she pretty much threw me out of her office when she took my temperature and it was quite a way over 100 degrees Fahrenheit. I hadn't had much of a fever the entire time, and that thermometer reading didn't just scare her, it terrified me. To be told at that point it was now rising was not what I had gone there to hear. I went home to my apartment, sat on my terrace on what was a beautiful spring day and cried. I had become terrified by the doctor's demeanor, fearing I was in the danger zone and probably about to die, until my father reminded me to take a few slow deep breaths. Then take some more. My lungs were still okay, I thanked God, and that reality helped loosen the tentacles of fear I had let tighten around my entire body on my way home from the doctor's office. I took another, nice deep breath, filling my lungs back up as I thanked my dad for staying close these last eleven years since he'd died; these last six months since September when something had died inside me that morning I melted down, but most especially, these last few weeks with this virus, the one that was showing the world that, as we need to distance ourselves physically from others, the emotional closeness we can nurture, even in our separation, is as critical a life force. At that moment, a bright yellow plane heading in for a landing at LaGuardia *just happened, coincidentally,* to fly right over my terrace at that moment. The bold, black letters standing out magnificently, SPIRIT. *Thank you, Daddy. I love you too.*

I receive an email from Spiritual Cinema Circle. It was a bit of a surprise because I'd discontinued my membership not long before feeling it was necessary financially at the time. It was a farewell message from Stephen Simon, the founder. Not a personal goodbye to me in response to my communication to them about my decision to cancel, but because he had decided on "closing the circle," shutting down the company. I was sad, even though touched to have been included in the blast that had gone out to members. I'll admit, I had a flash of fear reading his goodbye message, given the virus that had invaded my body at that time. But it overtook me in the most beautiful way quite quickly: Stephen, with a ph, not a v, and also a last name that also happens to start with an S too, and it flipped beautifully, just like that . . . a reminder *he will always love us and be with us.* It was as if Stephen Simon *and* my dad Stephen Shurina both heard everything I'd been praying about just moments before that email arrived in my inbox.

Childhood came front and center in my mind, again, as *Charlotte's Web* crossed my heart again. As I watched movie after movie while on bedrest, trying to keep my mind calm while my heart waited for the moment I would wake drenched in sweat, unable to breathe, and have to leave my boys for the hospital, where I would probably die too, one of my most favorite books as a young girl was brought magically to life in a movie remake. Watching not only soothed my mind . . . but brought much peace to my panicked heart. It reminded me it was there, my love for it, way back then. Death. New life. True love. Magnificent spectacular fantastical stuff, even if it broke my heart after filling it so full as a young girl I felt it would burst. The day after I watched it, I ordered the book. An early birthday gift for myself. As I unwrapped it from the used bookseller I bought it from, the first thing I saw was the name "Stevens" scribbled across the side pages. And, after thanking my dad for letting me know he was right there with me, watching over me, I smiled again when I went straight to the last page, something I still love to do, and saw the words. Still my favorite place, whether book or song or movie screen . . . "The End." Somehow, someway, in that moment I was calmed. I knew, I just knew, this wasn't my end.

My father's eleven year anniversary, April 11, is upon me when the movie *Big* comes front and center in my mind and I decide to watch it. The love connection Tom Hanks and Elizabeth Perkins characters share made my heart melt. Another one of those *best love stories ever* for me, even if they don't wind up together at the end of that film, because it is brimming with hope and faith that maybe, just maybe, *what if* . . . those ten years later that the character Susan wonders aloud about actually come true and she and Josh get to be together again? To see such a pivotal scene between them playing out at Rye Playland, which is *coincidentally* Mac's home hockey rink, a place, and a boardwalk I've been blessed to be many times these last few years, reinforced the spectacular magnitude of this love story as Josh tells his Susan he has a million reasons to go back but only one to stay. And I return to the most beautiful tears as I remembered my own *what if* as I struggled to end my marriage. *What if* someone had only one reason to go . . . the most important one . . . they wanted to? *What if* someone had a million reasons to stay, but stayed true to the one that mattered most . . . they didn't want to. And I feel such gratitude for the gift I was given, the choice I chose, some may say foolishly, especially given the way these last few years have played out, but I feel it again oh so beautifully.

* * *

I stay quarantined, resting, and my heart begins to slow and my health begins to improve.

But it's Oprah and Deepak's meditations that save me.

One day they brought a vision of my old friend Bridget, paralyzed from her neck down since high school, and one of her inspirations, Christopher Reeve, front and center in my mind, along with something he once said: "Once you choose hope, anything is possible." She and I had agreed many more times than once after her accident, any morning may be the one you wake up and walk. Any moment might be the one where you stand up from your wheelchair. Any minute, everything can change. We both held onto that hope. We both kept that faith.

* * *

I had chosen hope, one day, along my way, and somewhere along that way, I'm not exactly sure exactly when, or where, I chose to unchoose it. I don't remember anything at all about the specific day it happened, what I was wearing, or what I may have had for dinner that day, but one day, probably after slipping away little by little, poof, it was gone.

I'm reminded of this beautiful quote that brims with such brightness and lightness at the end of a tunnel that helps keep us moving toward our dreams, yet if allowed to flip can feel quite a turnaround in a dark abysmal cave ... nothing changes, nothing changes, nothing changes, then everything changes. I googled it recently wanting to give proper credit to another tiny bit of assistance that has helped keep my head above the water when I felt like I was drowning off the shores of that unprotected Sandy Hook beach I decided to dive into. I discovered it is attributed to the Greek philosopher Heraclitus's words that encourage us to actively participate in the changes of our lives, rather than letting change dictate it. As I saw that I'll admit I smiled, sinking into the memory of a private bucket-list trip I'd shared with only a special chosen few, a Mediterranean cruise to explore the ancient ruins. As I immersed myself in that memory, I became aware something beautiful was changing even if I wasn't fully aware of what exactly was morphing and transforming. But I knew I was on my way somewhere that felt good and positive again, co-creating with life again, being reminded that hope, and love too, will guide us, if we let it. It helped reconnect me to the Universe I'd trusted I'm one with, and the God inside me. When I finally, fully, started swimming in that truth again it rippled out and changed my life. As I take hold of it once again as I pray to survive Covid, I renew my trust in that wave.

*　*　*

A few months later and fall has arrived—I was full throttle trying to heal not just emotionally and mentally but physically too as the virus seemed to have some exhausting lingering effects on my body. Healing was slow while I worked long hours at a warehouse overloaded with shipments as many people remained housebound because of virus restrictions. My body felt weak. I wasn't able to muster my usual love for my favorite holiday Thanksgiving, and with many still home because of the restrictions, many Amazonians worked even harder to keep up with the demands of online ordering.

Long hours standing on a hard concrete floor, coupled with extra shifts to make up for the money I lost while out with the virus had caused me to fall even further behind in my finances. And of course my physical exhaustion overtired my mental and emotional bodies. But, my dad found a way to gift a little lift.

The owl is my spirit animal, or at least that's what a quiz told me long ago, along with a trusted intuitive mentor telling me the same not so long ago. Rocky, the owl who'd somehow made its way with the Rockefeller Center Christmas tree on a grueling trek after it had been cut down and transported into New York City, had just been set free to continue its journey, hopefully a less arduous one, after being nursed and tended to until it was strong enough to fly on its own again after workers had found the owl when unpacking the tree. It was assumed it was male when it was named, yet he turned out to be a she, which was a wink and a nod from my father for sure, after watching my own grueling trek and well aware *Rocky* is one of my favorite movies and love stories; he knew I would get the click and connection immediately. He knew how much I needed a hand on my own trip, in my own love story about underdogs, and sent me my very own underowl to remind me, *Hold your form, Tia.*

Mental, Emotional Meet Physical

Every tragedy of the human experience can be attributed to one human decision—the decision to withdraw from one another.
—Neale Donald Walsch

Hold my form, I did, eventually getting well enough to get back to my favorite endorphin-releasing pastime to free the anguish that ailed me.

And, as always, music continued to move me on my runs. Running with my music helps me stay in tune with my life. Literally. As I pound the pavement, I remember how important music can be when I'm feeling pounded by life off those running trails. It allows me to take inspiration beyond my earphones even after I take them off. The words, the lyrics, the lines all help me do just that when I move in other areas of my life besides the bike trails. When lyrics touch me, I move them into every part of my life. When Meghan Trainor reminds me we never know when we'll run out of time, I return in a split second to my sprint through the Sarasota airport to make it to my father in time. When Tracy Byrd croons about his lover being his fingers when he wants to feel, God do I desire to be the reason someone feels *that*. After Elvis asked me during a very private date to take his hand—I not only held it tight, I offered my whole life up as well so deeply had I been touched, so magically had I been moved by his lyrics. My music, the melodies, the lyrics, they all help me when the dance floor that is the real life ground we move and groove on every day gets scary, intimidating, overwhelming.

Running—and the accompanying music—had saved me so many times and in so many ways throughout this time, but I had somehow managed to ignore the vehicle that did the actual running. Dealing with a knee getting tighter and tighter with every run and now round of my bike pedals could involve any number of physical afflictions, but I knew each would include stopping both my beloved running and cycling for some time, and I just couldn't do it. Nor would I consider another shot of cortisone like I'd done years earlier, afraid it would haywire my heartbeat again. The higher powers, however, knew it was time. After running myself into the ground in every part of my life for these last ten years, my body literally had done the same. After feeling truly stuck, locked in an excruciating limbo for years, my leg locked and really stopped moving.

I awoke one morning after two days of long runs and bike rides to a leg blown up twice its usual size, swollen stiff, a couple degrees shy of a 180-degree position. God stopped me in my tracks, literally, with a very tough whack with the proverbial 2x4 to get my attention since I hadn't listened to their whispers to take better care of myself. Albert Einstein reminded me many times that "life is like riding a bicycle. To keep balance you must keep moving." But I had blurred an awful lot of lines trying to convince myself I was actually moving, in an effort to keep the balance.

There's a small wooden sign, sandwiched between sketches of my grandparents, hanging on the dining room wall in my seaside bungalow that reads, "When in doubt, look up." It caught my eye as I tried to make my way around after finally maneuvering out of my bed, still in a state of panic, confusion, and complete and total stun that I couldn't actually walk, nevermind run. In that instant I said a prayer to them, and anyone else up there who might be listening, followed by a favorite mantra, *I trust you.* Somehow in that moment it clicked . . . as I had made my way to trusting God above all in my life before, I had begun to trust my own self more. And, I acknowledged, out loud, even in the sheer terror of the moment, I was being gifted that opportunity again. And with each breath after, another tiny shuffle, not even able to babystep at that point, I knew I was on a critical crossroad leading me to a major turning point in my story, even if I had no idea what was about to unfold before me. The switch was flipping, finally, and at the same time, a lightbulb began brightening. All this angst, all this anxiety . . . it has been trying to tell me something is not right in my life . . . *what am I going to do about it?!*

The Universe let me know I did indeed see the light in that remembrance of self, in that beautiful moment of surrender, when it gave me a graceful gift of good news to hold onto. Not too many days later I received word that my goddaughter, who'd been in Europe for a soccer tryout, had signed a contract to play for Hungary. My dad, watching from above as his granddaughter would play her next season as a professional athlete, was smiling for sure, over the sun and the moon in happiness for her. Really, truly, above them, from heaven. And he was helping his daughter keep faith in all of them up there at the same time. This force that created galaxies, this power that powered life itself, surely they could handle this problem with my knee . . . or at least get me through what was to come with its mending. Trusting that, and the gods, my guides, all the angels, along with my paternal grandmother, who was Hungarian by the way, helped that to happen for my goddaughter Marianna Grace over July 29 . . . 729, my dad's favorite number (and also just happens to be my goddaughter's birthday). Their wink and nod makes me weep even to this day.

I would eventually wind up in the operating room five times over the next seven months. My first wake up from anesthesia in the recovery room had me wailing in a pain neither the nurses nor my doctor could make sense of or alleviate. They had filled me to the max with the strongest possible painkillers to try and make me more comfortable yet I cried out in a pain that had my body shaking uncontrollably and it concerned the team of caregivers around me very much. Four more trips later, I no longer need Fentanyl to jumpstart my day but I do pop an Advil some mornings to help maneuver my way through the pain (even if I am learning more and more each and every day the damage they are doing to my insides as a consequence to that alleviation).

So many months with my one leg immobile placed significant stress on my back and spine as I literally had to lug the healing limb around, lifting it as I swung it around and forward with every step. My movement was so restricted, so challenging, that I had to stop taking the escalators on the subway as it was too dangerous trying to sync with the moving stairs to get on and off. The strain on my body climbing the flights of stairs, since most times the elevators in the subway system were out of service for one reason or another, was enormous. My neck had long been an issue, a contributing factor to my migraines which I'd gotten under control due in part to regular adjustments to my atlas and axis regions. But the gait I walked with from midsummer 2021 into another new year completely disjointed me and did extensive damage.

Chiropractic care became a rare treat for me those last couple of years, so the assistance it could provide was minimal; I was severely limited in my ability to afford that form of treatment at the time. I may not have known the cause of why such a physical form of assistance was rendered restricted to me at a time it seemed I needed it most, but I was able to hold onto a truth that it wasn't because of anything I had done wrong, nor was God behind it in any punishing way. God was, in fact, very much watching over me, guiding me, in the most blessed way. That faith, hope, and optimism helped me stay focused on the treatments that were possible for me, and covered by my insurance, rather than get sidetracked by the slowdown that would happen if I let my worries and wonders and "why me's" push me along my road of rehabilitation. And as I struggled to get back my physical health, my financial health took another slide as those few months turned to well over a year out of work and my real-life angel became Larry, helping me to make many copays and supporting me with other critical necessities as I struggled to heal my knee.

My orthopedic surgeon shared the standard and normal time for a knee replacement is approximately one to three hours. He told me mine went much longer because my knee was so destroyed, resulting in even more complications and in addition to the normal side effects to deal with due to the anesthesia extension and blood flow restriction. He had shared his professional opinion before the surgery that he wasn't sure how much the knee replacement would return its ability to bend. He was sure he could get some slight flexion back, but how much more than just a few degrees . . . he had no idea, and didn't want to get my hopes up. I had let it go untreated for so long that he just wasn't able to give much of a promising prognosis. He said the best determination for doctors about how their patients will heal is the condition those patients are in when they perform the surgery. My case couldn't have been much worse, he was sorry to inform me. I, on the other hand, had some very high hopes and broke down as I begged him to please help me hold onto them. He reassured me he would do his best in what he called my Hail Mary pass.

The day of surgery, when he stopped by before to say hello and see how I was doing with the pre-surgery prep, I gave him a gift; a small stuffed football. My father signed a contract to play baseball and pitch for the Cincinnati Reds but his first love was football. Even though I *knew* he was with me every step since his death, in my darkest moments, when the doubt and despair felt almost too much to handle, he always found a way to make sure I didn't forget it. I wanted to honor that and let my dad know I trusted the big picture he could see from his very divine vantage point. I told the doctor he couldn't throw a Hail Mary pass without a football so I was hoping he would take it into the OR with him. He smiled. I also told him even though I knew I was in good hands, he was going to have a lot of company in there with him, and I hoped he didn't mind, and he was so humble, and gracious, and open hearted as he assured me he welcomed the company, and the assistance.

He would eventually tell me post-op the damage was so extensive inside it looked like a soldier who had been through a war, or an athlete at the end of a very long career, as he explained the details of a case he'd never seen so extreme. He asked his PA, who also sat in the exam room, as well as in the OR with us, to confirm all of what he was sharing about the operation. It was as if things were so unbelievable, even to him, that he needed the back up to reassure both of us. Despite the extent of the damage, and every visit thereafter, he was so encouraging as I sat on the exam table holding back tears, in fear the flexion that was barely progressing in physical therapy would reverse and go back to being stuck straight as a pin again. The leg cramps that would wake me up at night could keep me up for hours, rippling out to include my feet and toes that would curl and clamp tight and leave me crying out in pain as I babystepped around my apartment in the dead of night trying to stop the spasming.

Even as I was discouraged by my progress, this special doctor, the second opinion I eventually made my way to, helped me to accept it really was quite extraordinary. His words not mine, which melted my heart and helped me to stand up and give him another hug. Even though I may never be able to ride a bike again, even if I may never be able to go for a run again, it was extraordinary nonetheless given the prognosis he had feared could be my future . . . spending the rest of my life lugging around a leg that wouldn't bend. And I am so indebted to that doctor for everything he did. His expertise and experience, along with his kind demeanor, his bedside manner and his open-mindedness to not just hearing me out, was a gift in itself. But, an even more precious present he gave was his listening to me as I shared my own thoughts and wonders about this important joint and all the possible backstories that attributed to the problem.

He listened to my fears and my hopes for my future, and his patience with my questions was remarkable, his assurance of an open office door to me anytime I wanted or needed to stop in for a check in, or look at, as long as he was physically there to see me, and if not gave me his word he would get right back to me, reading the metaphysical literature I shared with him to help him get inside my mind, my heart, and my soul, as he prepared to go inside my leg, all helped me turn a much needed corner during a very pivotal time so I wouldn't wind up heading back down an unhealthy path. The examples he used to describe the state of my knee connected some divine dot, the best kind of dots to use for me. His analogies reminding me of Sam, my US Marine, and Mac, my hockey player. That good doctor couldn't have found a more perfect way to help me hold onto faith that everything unfolding gives me an opportunity to take another step towards that which is in my highest and best good. That highest and best potential . . . part of a divine plan I did not create in my humanness.

I could have easily flipped a switch at that time and headed back in reverse again. But as I thought back upon Dr. D's words, some sacred dots connecting helped me consider my future. That holy hindsight helped me see the sacred foresight that helped me flip an unsatisfying life and create a new one for myself once again. A change I'd longed for quite a long while in my life.

And thanks to another good doctor, with his assistance, I found not just a blessing but a joy, which allowed me to begin drinking from a cup again that did not feel half empty. It wasn't half full either. It was overflowing again. I was alive. And I could walk. And even though every step I took was with a very uneven gait, I grew a little stronger and steadier everyday. And I just know that fullness will stay, even if that limp never goes away.

* * *

While I was housebound recuperating I got hooked on a couple shows as I rested after the extensive physical therapy I was doing each day. I'm not much of a TV watcher but it helped me stay put and pass the time while my body healed. *Beyond the Edge* introduced me to a coach I'd never heard of, Mike Singletary. He and another contestant, Ray Lewis, a former professional athlete like my dad, formed a bond that made quite an impression on me as I could almost hear my father's voice through their conversations. There is no doubt in my mind my dad was behind my decision to tune into this new show after scrolling around the guide and the channels for something to rest my body, and my mind, from the physical pain and exhaustion I felt. I also got to know a side of Paulina Porizkova I'd never seen, not that I knew her at all. But the self she showed the world in those episodes, with all her hip issues and joint problems, I fell madly in love with while watching her recommit and remain devoted to staying *in the game*. Mike's, Ray's, and Paulina's All-Ins all continued to inspire mine as I struggled to heal not just my knee, but my life. Again. Thank you, Dad. I love you too.

Another divine timing and unexpected assistance during my rehab, the last season of *This Is Us*. A wink and nod in hindsight I was on the right track when I decided to watch—realizing later that it had premiered on the same date of my surgery. I knew of the show, and had seen an episode early on, the one where the father dies from complications sustained in a fire. Who knows why I never tuned in again, maybe because of what my own dad had gone through in the FDNY, even though he survived the fire he fell into. But, all these seasons later it seemed it might just be the right and perfect timing as I was hooked one night while icing my knee, and was so drawn in I caught up on prior seasons during the days in between. As I watched Rebecca in the finale start her journey through the train cars, moving through the times and relationships of her life, I flashed back as well. I hobbled into my dining room during a commercial break, where an immense, handmade, beautifully crafted frame held a bulletin board, mirrored panels, and magnetic tin tiles that take up half of one whole wall. It was 1989 again in the snap of a finger, and I was dancing with my dad at my wedding to Paul Anka's "Times of Your Life." I fast forwarded a decade in the blink of my eye as pages from a calendar passage moved me, then and now. It was a two-page piece that started on December

30, 1998, named, "The Station," which ended the next day, New Year's Eve. It couldn't have been a more appropriate day or a more beautiful way to bolster my trust; a new beginning had begun with that New Year's January surgery. The passage is long, and my space here short, but I'll share that Robert J. Hastings's eloquent expression didn't just move me to tears that day in 1998 but took me to my knees again that night (well, metaphorically since kneeling still remained outside my realm of possibility). In two small calendar pages he took me on the train ride of life, inspiring me to embrace the trip *through* it, not what was waiting at the end of it. In a few short paragraphs he inspired me to relish the moment, not let fear or regret rob us of today since "the station" constantly outdistances us. That New Year's Eve reminder so many years ago helped me continue to babystep a beautiful path I had begun by then. And on this night, Kevin, Sophie, Rebecca, and Robert all inspired me to leap again.

And, as I leap, I keep firm faith in the inspiration from Sara Evans's "Pray for You" that we put on my dad's prayer card—that what will be, will be. I trust that now, again, with every fiber of my being, a being that now includes a titanium knee, along with a new team of doctors. A knee that still hasn't broken 80 degrees yet, post surgery, but I pray, someday, will. And a heart full of joy to read that *he* did in fact, finally break 80 in his golf game during the time my knee became unable to break any degrees as it locked in a 180 degree straight line. A prayer to give everything I'd learned and earned on my journey to *him*, to help him get where he wanted to go, offered up long ago . . . quietly, privately, purely, intently . . . prayed with every part of my being, answered as profoundly and powerfully as my desire. What a gift the gods have given me as they answered it. A high only able to experience because I let myself go as low. A clarity only able to become aware again because I had allowed confusion. A heart broken . . . open.

And staying open. Again. A love story really, truly, out of this world. And what a wonderful one here on earth as well. That faith, along with hope and love, sacred keys I carry with me, same as were when I found the blessing with Larry and our marriage and used those keys to open some new doors after finally closing some others. Different ones, but all, hallowed. No matter how scared I ever get, however hard I hit the walls, whatever ways I cross those doorways, whether I crawl, walk, run, bike, or hop skip and jump into my future, I move with the answer to a very special question I wondered to *him* privately so many years ago, then shared publicly for him years later in my first book *Everything and a Happy Ending* after flipping head over heels over my handlebars not long after I fell head over heels in love . . . "Would I have someone to help me if I fell when I was an old lady? I thought I was going to die that day, just like the actress Natasha Richardson died a year before after taking a tumble on the ski slope and hitting her head. My dad and I had a powerful conversation about life and death, timing, and things that were meant to be after her tragic accident, only months before my dad would pass over himself. I was very afraid that day."

The answer, encircling me now. By my side. Below me, behind me, in front of me. On top of me. All around me. *Again.* After facing my fears in my mirror again after book one was published, I have been reminded, once you know something, you can never un-know it. *Would I have someone to help me if I fell when I was an old lady?* I would. I did. I do. God. The same Universe waiting for me all those years and mini-lifetimes ago when I began my search for him. She's still there. They really do exist.

Mending, Bending, Rounding, and Re-Rounding

And this is what a goodbye should be. Not a period. But an ellipsis, a statement trailing off, until someone is there to pick it up.
—V. E. Schwab

Bob, the bartender at The Chubby Pickle, picked up right where me and my dad had left off. Our connection was that fast, and that easy. It was as if my dad put him right in my path during what felt like the most troubling time of my life. Bob was the typical cliché and assistance . . . kind and chatty when I'd stop by after a long run and bike ride; season after season as I tried to enjoy the journey, as difficult a time as it was, but he was never nosy, nor prying.

We read about it and hear it preached all the time: *Enjoy the journey, not just the destination! Find the gift! Feel gratitude and appreciation, even amidst our struggles!* It's a message so important that it's plastered on magnets that are then plastered all over refrigerators everywhere. It had taken me a long mini-life to find the blessing of my marriage and feel gratitude and appreciation for it. It was only when I found it, I found the peace that had been the missing piece in my struggle to end it. And I was losing my thankfulness again, for so much and so many things that I couldn't seem to find or feel anymore. As Oscar Wilde reminded my heart though, "What seems sometimes are our most bitter trials are blessings in disguise," my body was beginning to weaken as I clung to that hope.

Bob, who I barely knew, but who knew so much about so much, helped extend the high the miles of running and biking had just helped with as he extended his hand in friendship (and Bloody Mary!). So stereotypical but so spot on—barman by morning with ears that loved to listen, doubling as a big ole breathing, walking, talking encyclopedia of obscure knowledge that could enlighten and entertain his customers. My dad had bartended, besides driving a cab, sandwiched in between construction work after his fire related injuries forced him to retire from the FDNY, so I think he touched a soft spot for me, wondering what *his* backstory might be. Years later, long after I knew a little of it, and our friendship had grown, when I would spend the summer healing after five trips to the OR during the prior fall and winter it would be Bob who would keep me on track, helping support me as I limped around town.

"Yo, Gimpie, so good to see you coming along." "Yo, Gimpie, you're doing great." "Yo, Gimpie, when you gonna start running again?" To which I'd holler back across Bay Avenue or chuckle across the bar, "God only knows, Bob, only God knows my friend!"

Heath Ledger's words had hit hard on some of the difficult days. "Your biggest supporter is a stranger. Your biggest hater is someone you know." *Hater* may be too strong a word for my own personal story. *Holder backer* might better convey the sentiment and spirit that resonates in my experience. So many holder backers . . . "family," "friends"—who I feel quite certain would have liked nothing better than for me to stay right where I was. But not Bob. I thanked God, and my father, for him many times these last few years.

He liked to write . . . and read. As a nonprofessional writer who'd somehow managed to write a book, I knew nothing about either of those worlds, and he generously shared with me all his "stuff." He suggested I go to the Literary Club in NYC. I haven't yet. He suggested I read "A Rose for Emily." I haven't yet. He introduced me to Willa Cather as well as a local customer, a friend he thought might like to read my book—a single mom struggling to make some difficult choices in her life. At last check she hadn't read it yet, but like me, I trust will get to it when it's the right and perfect time for her. He shared his daughter's touching Father's Day note beaming with pride while watching me read her loving words of tribute. We went from barkeep and customer to buddies, such a beautiful thing to me. He was the perfect person to follow my runs as that Oscar Wilde quote became harder to cling to. While some shared their thoughts thoughtfully, others, nowhere near ruminatively, Bob became a safe haven in a storm of voices I was trying desperately to shut out. There was nothing I wouldn't do, to stay true, to my All-In—*no mountain too high, no valley too low*. When a song streamed from the speakers as I was hugging my goodbye to Bob one day I couldn't help but sit back down on the barstool and go back in time for a boost of faith before heading back out into the challenge of a very clouded day.

* * *

I will never forget hearing Diana Ross sing "Ain't No Mountain High Enough" live. It was a deluge of emotion that mixed with a rain storm so powerful it would send the entire Great Lawn of Central Park pouring onto the New York City streets surrounding it one summer night in the early '80s, just before I would wind up moving out of the family apartment because I'd *"grown up"* (or so my father said I had) after he angrily told me it was time to move out. Diana wouldn't leave the stage at first. And all of us stayed right there with her. As it rained. Then poured. The sky filling with thunder and lightning. What a concert! What a love! For her fans, the music. *One no wind, no rain, nothing could stop.* The confluence of intensity and intimacy I witnessed and was a part of that evening, the energy that enveloped me, the feeling that filled me . . . that memory has never left me—it was so beautiful to be swept up in such emotion. It was surreal, yet so very real. And even though I love the surreal, I find it sublime most times, this feeling that continued growing inside as I tried to hold on to faith and hope in the life I promised my dad I would stay true to, I didn't love at all. I was reminded of that as the song ended and I was overcome with fraught about getting up from that barstool, knowing somewhere deep inside the struggle to take those lyrics into my real life was intensifying. Even if I knew not what exactly was going on and changing, I did know it was feeling less good as the calendar pages continued turning quietly, with no word, still, waiting for another to let me know what I was supposed to be doing with my future. I signed my book to Bob's single mom friend with an encouragement to make the changes she was so wanting to make in her life for *herself* more than anyone else, even though my own self had by now long put another firmly in front of me by that point. Something was missing again in my life. And what was missing . . . was me, even if at the time I refused to consider that, never mind accept or embrace it. But, Bob's gentle presence was instrumental in helping me to eventually finally face that difficult truth.

Marie

———— ✦ ————

Our family often teaches us our biggest soul lessons—the most important
karma we're here to work on this lifetime.
—DailyOM course, *"Release Yourself from Family Karma"*

S ince most of my first book, and much of this second, was written
on what was her front porch, beside her beautiful garden filled
with old Mother's Day gifts of pink hydrangea plants, in a tiny tweak
of Alice Walker's beautiful quote, "In search of my [grand]mother's
garden, I found my own"—I'd like to tell you a little bit about Marie
Murphy Mahoney. And not least because when I came out of the hospital, after those darkest days and when I had been set on my path of
healing, I began writing again, and writing about Marie was a calling
that I couldn't ignore.

* * *

I love alliteration. Such a graceful flow for words. My grand-mother's probably the reason why. And, she's also probably part of the reason I struggled with a very ungraceful feeling when I was a young woman. As I've devotedly tried to swim with the current of my life these last ten years, I've thought often of her devotion to *not* going with the flow of her life—a way of life I think she was so deeply committed to.

With her grandkids, she was adoring. She doted on us, watched over us, took care of us. She loved to sing to us, adored to draw and sketch for us, showered us with attention, and affection, as she stuffed our bellies, our hearts, and our brains, when we were with her. To this day, I still address my boys sometimes as doll, or dolly, a term of endearment she used all the time with her grandchildren. When she had a few beers and tomato juices, she was even more gaga for us. I felt safer with her than most for much of my childhood. But I felt an utter sadness as well, though, when around her. I didn't know why when I was younger. I knew she loved us, but the apparent loathing of her own self, along with others in the family circle around her, seemed to seep out of her as much and as often as the adoration for her grandchildren oozed out; it was very confusing.

It was a stark contrast, difficult to understand in my youth and teenage years. It was only after she passed, and I grew into my own womanhood, that I could start to make some sense of that disparity. Just like with me and my dad, as we matured, we started the process to see things from a different perspective, and then, in those new eyes, chose to transform our relationships. But while she was alive, while she was a safe light for me, at the same time she did have a lot of darkness in her that would help make my own light a little difficult to see at times, never mind let shine.

She slept in the dining room of her apartment on a single bed that doubled for something to sit on while at the table. For holidays, the living room would transform into the dining space. My grandmother would do everything—no one would bring anything from what I remember, and she would go all out.

Her life was about taking care of her family, and at the time she was living, that translated to food. It was almost all she had, I began to see as I looked back, years after she passed, and my heart began to break for her in a very different way than when I was younger. But while she was alive, she would make us plates of tuna and egg salad and call upstairs for one of us to come down and pick up. Whatever had been prepared was always perfect. And when she made her soups— heaven. Her pea soup was my favorite. She did it all for us. She really didn't have any other life from what I could see. I don't remember her working, volunteering, going out with friends—except the small handful at Honeysuckle Lodge where my grandparents would spend two months each summer, leaving apartment life in Queens for a shack on the Jersey shore—or having one outside interest, other than church on Sundays. We would always go with my grandparents. Some Sundays she would let me wear her costume jewelry—big necklaces with a matching broach, bracelet and ring, which were always worn together—the style at the time. She loved to draw and was a talented artist. It seemed enough for her. *Maybe.* Turns out it probably, in fact, I'm almost sure of it, wasn't. It might have been real but I'm not sure it was completely true because she would so often complain about it. *Someone outside of herself* was *causing her* to be unhappy. My grandfather would top that list, followed by my dad, a very close second. There were others—anyone who wasn't treating one of her children the way she felt they *should* be treated or behaving differently than she wanted, because, as I would come to understand, it was her who was not living up to her own standard. I think she knew inside but felt stuck between the woman she kept in there and the one she showed others. The woman she wanted to be, and the one the world expected her to be . . . the wife, the mother, the grandmother. That's the way it was then. Whether the woman she was had been in conflict or strife or depressed emotionally or off balance mentally, not content because of her circumstances or struggled with some real chemical or physiological or biological challenges that exacerbated some of those states of being, or some combination of, I do not know. There was not the same attention or talk of such things then as now, and certainly much more of a stigma attached to mental health issues. A paternal aunt died in a psychiatric hospital and my father said it was an absolute taboo subject in his family. Rumor had it she was a closeted lesbian, but of course it was never confirmed. It was *not* to be spoken of. *So* much secrecy about *so* much stuff so much of the time. Opening the door for discussion opens many more doors on the road to our best health. It's a complicated issue, for sure, and each person's journey is their own. It can be overwhelming as we each try to live our life, diagnosing our issues and ailments, then deciding what treatments and assistance speak clearest and best to us. Simple sounding stuff that is sometimes quite complicated, often daunting to make our ways through. I have to accept I won't know with any certainty until I get to the other side about all that was going on inside her while she was alive, but I can get clear and do my best to remain in clarity about my own while I'm here now, so I don't just survive but thrive in ways I don't think she felt or thought she could.

When we were at those food fests on the holidays, down having dinner with her during the week, or even when she would call us upstairs to come pick up whatever food she'd prepared for us, she would usually use that time *after* to complain about it. She would almost always find a way to take some of the joy right out of it, almost in direct proportion to all that love she had just put into it, by criticizing, berating, someone or something that was somehow related to that very meal she had just spent her time lovingly preparing. She could always find a six degrees of separation between them. Besides her standard question, which makes me laugh now, but then it scared me so, and was so embarrassing, "Did you move your bowels today?" her way of checking on our well-being, which she was certain was not being tended to properly, and expressed, often, there was a whole host of questions and topics and people she would *let her stuff out* about.

Venting, or vomiting your *stuff* out onto others can be a fine line that is easy to blur. It wouldn't be during the big dinners that were well attended, because to be honest, I don't even remember her being at the table for them. She was always moving back and forth between the kitchen and living room for something or someone at the table. Maybe she would sit for a minute, but then she'd be gone, back in the tiny kitchen. More butter, someone dropped their fork, the bowl of potatoes needed replenishing. Or maybe there was just no space to fit her. Or maybe she didn't even set a place for her own self when she put together the table where everyone else was about to sit at and enjoy . . . the conversation, the laughter, the love, all *the good stuff* that Kenny Chesney sings about that's supposed to fill us and our lives . . . *isn't it?* I don't know. All I do know was it was standard and normal for her to not even be enjoying the event, the meal, just making sure it was by others. It would show, though, during the cleanup, when she was in the kitchen washing all the dishes, maybe even with a few beer and tomato juices that was one of her treats for herself, when it would emerge. And after the smaller dinners at the kitchen table or when we would be the messenger that would go pick up the daily goodies when some standard and usual questions could ripple into a third degree. *Did you eat anything else today? Where is your father today? How is your mother? Have you done your homework? Did you take a shower? Is everything okay upstairs? Do you need anything? Does your mother need money?* And my favorite, amidst all the humiliating, intrusive questions, that I know now weren't ever meant to hurt me, nor especially not her own daughter but I feel strongly probably must have demeaned her, very much, there was one request I loved, even if I knew it would mean more interrogation I was afraid to answer for fear of upsetting someone, saying the wrong thing, giving the wrong reply . . . *Why don't you stay and have some cookies or cake before you go back upstairs?* There was always Entenmann's pound cake, Planter's peanuts, and Lorna Doones. And oh my god, how I loved those Mister Salty pretzels. And, I could never leave out the Hershey's Kisses, Mary Janes, or Jell-O. They were the staples. I still drink buttermilk to this day. And she would love it when we would sit in the kitchen with her and watch TV with her on her little black-and-white, while my grandfather would watch *Lawrence Welk* or *All in the Family* in his recliner in the living room. Same shows but two different rooms. They didn't even watch TV together. And, sadly, there was no one there, or anywhere, who would explain it, ease the turmoil the mystery was creating, help make some sense of the tension that seemed to envelope our most sacred places . . . upstairs in 6-D, downstairs in 4-B.

When my grandfather went food shopping she would insist he was out flirting with all his girlfriends. And as he ran one errand after another, which he always seemed to do, while she always seemed to be home, she would play her records on the enormous record player in the living room. It was like a piece of furniture. It actually *was* a piece of furniture. A huge wooden hi-fi that held the record player and all their albums. It was bigger than even the TV. And I truly believe it was where she found her peace. She would listen to Perry Como or Dean

Martin or her favorite, Eddy Arnold. She liked him, as in *liked*, she shared once. A tiny little slip of a hidden crush and fantasy and a side to a woman rarely seen. She so enjoyed her time then, living a different life for herself. She came out of her shell more then. She talked more, complained less. Where she went, or what life she was living inside herself most days, I don't know, because she never shared it with me. Or anyone, I don't think. But it was in there. I just know it now. What a gift her sadness would eventually show me, teach me, present me with, give to me, about love, about life, about *self*. Her life held some happy times, but they were brief, and fleeting. *Joy*, however, had a hard time finding a place within her home.

Questioning more and more why she didn't seem able to notice the simple beauty of living helped me as I would wonder why my own wheels were spinning the way they were as I grew older. I shared in my first book how in high school one day a slip I was wearing slid down without me noticing and tripped me. I'm sure the elastic was long overstretched between me, my older sister, and my mom sharing it. I recounted how I felt sure every person who got off that bus with me was laughing at me. It took a long time, and a lot of soul searching to get to a place in my life where I understood it wasn't the actual incident that mortified me. It represented everything I felt necessary to hide about our family, our home, our life that I felt fell to the ground that day and was exposed for everyone to see, not the slip, or trip, itself. And, my gram helped me on that journey, to go, and grow, to that place I finally made it to, then made it *back again* . . . a place where I can laugh a little easier at some really, truly funny moments to balance a world that can be chock full of such painful un-funniness at times.

Even though her bed was in the dining room, her dresser was in their one bedroom. Which was meticulous, as was the apartment. At all times. Somehow, even when the apartment was crammed with people, everything remained in perfect order. Never a mess. Which was heaven to me. Our apartment upstairs was not only not in perfect order but a stark contrast most days. Her dresser was long, the darkest wood, almost black. Always with a delicate lace doily spread across the top daintily displaying some of her most treasured stuff, even if one of those prized possessions was a sewing kit. I still have it, an old Walkers shortbread tin, to sew up the rips and tears of others. That dresser was a long, holy altar to me—big, strong, and masculine yet with an oh-so-feminine mirror in the middle, her jewelry box center of it all. After she died, my grandfather let us each take something from it. I chose her rosary beads. When Larry and I moved into their apartment just before we married, I had the dresser sanded and made it my own. I would paint it white one day, and take it with me when we needed a bigger place. I still have that dresser . . . in the room where my bed is as well. It may be an empty king-size bed right now, but it is in the bedroom nonetheless, not the dining room, which I see as a huge step forward from my gram's life, and, I feel strongly, a step that has made her smile.

When she would get dressed up, oy, would she dress up. So much different than the housecoat she used to wear most days. I have a trophy that belonged to her and my grandfather. *Marie & John Mahoney. Peabody Champs 1962.* I think the only time I ever saw them touching was when they would dance at weddings or big family parties at the local Knights of Columbus hall, or out back at the cabana, behind their bungalow at the shore. I had no idea when we moved from my grandparents' apartment why that trophy was one of the very few things I wanted to take with me, but it has held a place of honor in my homes ever since. After *he* won a Peabody Award for the show that had been the bridge for us to cross together so we could fall in love, I could almost see Gram's beautiful blue-grey eyes bursting with sparks of light, as my heart burst with happiness for him, knowing why finally. Some may snicker at that notion, some may say it is just another coincidence. But for me, it is another winking and nodding from above, tiny dots connecting in a divine story written long ago, on the other side of heaven for two souls next human lives, if we would *choose* it for ourselves.

I still keep two bottles of her perfume in the bungalow. Both by Fabergé—Kiku and Aphrodesia. The names I would never remember if I didn't make labels for the small bottles I poured them into. But the scents, I could never forget. And I still stop a few times throughout the summer and open up the tops to get a whiff of her. She's been dead more than a few decades, but it's like she is standing right next to me when I close my eyes and take a deep breath.

* * *

She was a very different person with my dad than her grandkids. My gram made it loud and clear, time and again—my father was ruining my mother's life and was a poor excuse for a father to boot. I won't choose to share more than that a bookie chasing my dad over the 59th Street bridge with some of his kids in the car after a softball game in Central Park probably was *not* helpful to get her to see him in a different light, much as that was not the true man. I'm sure he felt a double whammy to feel so unloved by *both* his mothers.

After years of telling us she would be dead soon and we'd all be better off, diabetes eventually took her to the hospital she would die in. I went straight from my high school class after being told she wasn't getting any better. When I got there, and stepped into the reality of that room, I truly left a whole world behind me. She'd been on the heavier side most of my life, pleasantly plump, but certainly not obese, until the beginning of the end, when she would start thinning out. But, in that bed, on that day I saw a woman who had wasted away. She was so frail. She couldn't speak because there was something in her mouth, or covering it, I can't be completely certain, but she was conscious as she laid quietly. I was not only shocked but petrified seeing her like that. As I stood by the side of the bed, I could not utter a single word, even though inside I was so desperate to bare my soul and say so much. *I'm sorry. Please forgive me. I'll come down more. Don't die. Please don't die. I need you. Please. Thank you. Please don't leave me.* But, I couldn't get the words out, not one. Only tears came out. I was trying so hard not to cry, so as not to upset her, but hard as I tried to get words out, and keep the tears in, my mind, and my heart, would only allow the opposite. As I looked into her eyes, eyes we wouldn't take off each other for that brief visit, a gift I'm thankful for even if not a word was spoken, as the tears I was trying to hold back streamed down my cheeks, as I tried my best not to let that trickle turn to a tumble, and my nose just seemed to run, and run, right down, over my lips, and past my chin as I wouldn't move in those moments, the tiniest of tears escaped her left eye as well. I was standing to her left, and her head was tilted toward me, so the tears all seemed to come out that one eye. My left hand on top of her left hand, eyes locked, in my mind, along with my other words, begs, pleads, prayers, confessions, I said it over and over—*I love you, Gram. I love you. I love you.*

A beautiful thing to me to look back now on that memory with her and realize it mirrored, in the same exact way, some of my last moments with my dad, right down to the right of his bedside. My right hand placed on top of his right hand as my head was bowed, resting on his forearm, so deep in thought, and prayer, and tears, as I spoke with him in the privacy of my mind, and my heart. But there was one difference . . . no I'm sorrys, no please-forgive-mes, no regrets, no words left unsaid, just *the good stuff,* and a prayer for ease and grace, and as painless as possible, on his chosen journey, whatever that would be at that point. That difference—a gift from him through our newfound relationship—I will always be grateful for.

Complications from my grandmother's diabetes would eventually take her—while only in her sixties, when she had so much of life left to live, if only she had been in a place where she would *choose* that for herself. She didn't want to be *here,* but she wouldn't go anyplace else for herself. She just stayed in place, afraid to step out of a life in which she felt stuck. Maybe because she didn't have any idea where she might actually go, although I just don't know. I think of Alex Borstein's passionate plea to women at the 2019 Emmys as she shared her story of her own grandmother. Two grandmothers' lives on the line, really, in completely different ways, of course, but on the line nonetheless. One, as Alex shared through her story, too afraid to *not* step out of line at the concentration camp she was in, on her way to certain death. And another grandmother, mine, too afraid to. One wanted to live. One willed herself to die. And then I thought of my own self. Too afraid to step out of line again, even with my own life on the line in so many important ways, yet stepping out of line in so many other unhealthy ways that were killing me as well. Just like with Larry, living a life that was hurting me in so many ways because I was so afraid of hurting in other ways. This was such a moment of clarity for me, seeing how my grandmother *chose* to stay stuck and that I didn't, at first. And in reflecting on my grandmother, I had to acknowledge that after all the work I had done after my dad passed that I then returned right back to that place in my pain and confusion over *him,* convincing myself my actions were justified, needed, *whatever* . . . rather than face the fact I was avoiding so much by justifying it all. Avoiding it so much that it landed me in the psyche ward—a truly literal push to get me on the path where I could begin to heal and mend and attempt to break the cycle yet again. All of this gives me more validation of the power of our thoughts. And even more about the importance of our feelings.

Mom

Only a person who risks is free.
—William Arthur Ward, *"To Risk"*

Turns out most of my 2023 was much like the last mile of the NYC Marathon I ran that fateful November. As I neared reentry into Central Park to end the run, it was my father I felt at my back as I made my way to that finish line. In 2023, it would be my mom who would carry me over the finish line of the year after the excruciating trek through those twelve months slammed me into an epic runner's wall. I included a favorite quote that both my dad and I loved from Deepak Chopra's *Golf for Enlightenment* in *EaaHE*. "Be of one mind. Let the swing happen. Find the now and you'll find your shot. Play from your heart to the hole." In 2023, it would be my mom who would make sure I stayed, and played, from the heart; my mom who would help me return to my faith in the divine blueprint of my life after it was almost entirely lost again, after she died at what felt the wrongest, most imperfect time in my life.

* * *

The way it had been in ours was unhealthy in some important ways. My mom, out of all of us, knew that best even if she would not face that truth at that time. We could change our relationship, but I could never go back. Now, as an adult in the havoc of my unwinding love story of all time, I begged her, opening up in ways I had never allowed myself before with her, vulnerably expressing what I wanted from her . . . her support, and I wanted her to stand in her own courage and stand up to some of my siblings.

My dad had been more than a bit of a bully in his younger years and the earlier example he had set was indeed a powerful one, which had affected his children and his wife in our own different ways. Her beg, "Just ignore it, let it go in one ear and out the other . . . like I do." Her plea, "Please, for me," after suggesting I get help to *accept* the strains that were paining my life rather than her offering her support to actually *deal with* those strains—and siblings. I challenged her when I replied, "Like the help you always got mom?" It was painful for her to hear, I knew that. And, it was as painful for me to say.

Her way was never discussed between us before some long-ignored childhood stuff came bursting out a few years after my dad died. But I wanted so much to be honest and authentic with her, the way my dad and I had chosen to be with one another in those last few years we had together. And what she was asking me to do at that moment in time, to stuff it back down, *accept* it all, specifically the way a few of my siblings were treating me, when we were both well aware it was not healthy, was something I would not do. I would not make the choice to allow it to rot me from the inside out which it would do if I ignored it all.

Honoring that decision brought peace, even amidst the great pain that was part of the process after the decision to distance myself from the dysfunction. She supported me in other ways that she was more able to, but in this most important way—acknowledging and having my back as I rode my rollercoaster ride with *him*—she just couldn't do. She was too afraid of the fallout; the results and reactions that would ripple outward from the already raging riptides wreaking havoc within our family. I will always be grateful for her help. But another part felt let down by her, as I had during some heartbreaking times in my younger years. I'm second oldest in the lineup but I very much took on many of the responsibilities of a first born in my younger years. I'd looked out for and watched over my siblings during some scary moments in our childhood and I wanted her support at this fearful time in my life. My consolation and compassion were found in a very real truth; she didn't have it within her own self, and she could never give to me what she was unable to give to herself. She had never stood up for her own self . . . how could she ever stand up for another?

I had such empathy for her struggles to overcome a lot of her own emotional trauma and baggage, but it was deeply hurtful at times, the distance that would eventually wind up between us, even though I know she loved me very much, as I did her.

* * *

It's January when my mom is taken by ambulance to the hospital. A simple hernia no one even knew existed—even if my mother had been eating less and less the last few years and, as a nurse herself, was probably very aware something was not right inside her. It had grown extensive, leaving my mother unable to nourish herself. It was sudden, scary, and treatment options were accompanied by controversy. My sister Susie, a nurse like our mom, was her chosen health care proxy. My mom wanted very much for the doctor to sign the release papers so she could go home and do the research she needed to do to make *her own* decision, which Susie agreed our mother should have the right to decide for herself what action to take. As my sisters' angry voices raised in my mother's hospital room, she turned to me and reached out her hand to come sit by her side. With arms locked and hands held tight we sat by the side of her bed, me trying to distract her. We talked privately, one mother to another. One daughter to another. One Patricia to another. In those few minutes she gifted me with one of my most revered presents, "Tia, *you* understand me."

* * *

By early March my mom was still not in the best of places, and when I received a message from my mom—not my baby sister Susie on her behalf, but a text directly from her—I should have known she was preparing for the next stage.

After I had returned to New York in January I had been keeping in daily touch with Susie for updates so my mom could concentrate on only one thing: strengthening her physical body before surgery. At some point I'd asked Susie if my mom wanted me to reach out to her two oldest and dearest friends from childhood. She hadn't told either yet and we thought it might be a good boost for her to talk with either, or both, Jimmy or John. When first asked, just before, then again just after the surgery, she said she wanted to feel stronger and healthier when she spoke with them and told Susie to tell me to hold off, but she would like me to when she was ready and would let me know when that time was. She trusted I would only reach out when she told me to, something she was not used to others in her orbit respecting . . . her want and will. And so when she was feeling a little firmer on her road to recuperating after the hernia surgery that had been deemed a success, albeit a much more complicated surgery than her doctor had been expecting that day on the OR table after explaining what would be an extensive repair, she decided she would like to speak with them.

She told Susie she wanted me to make the calls. I was back in New York and dialed both of them immediately. Not surprisingly, Susie, who was with my mom in her hospital room that day told me Jimmy and John each rang her phone seconds after hanging up with me and even though she left the room to give my mother privacy to speak with her old friends, my mom shared with her how happy the conversations made her. The text message my mother sent me just after those conversations was, and will always be, my most treasured gift from her: *Dear Tia, Thank you so much for opening the door to allow me to talk to my two very special friends. It was the best gift anyone could possibly give me.*

It's not too much later when Mac and I are set to make our way from New York to Florida to see her at the hospice she was moved to abruptly after a troubling turn of tides suddenly rerouted all of us, most especially my mom. Mac's alarm doesn't go off, and I send Susie ahead onto the plane for final boarding to join our nephew Ryan, who was already seated, as I stay behind, standing by the door of the gate, staying in touch with Mac, moving through security. As I beg the agent to hold the doors for another few moments, I flash back to my trip to Florida before my father died, making that flight by the skin of my teeth. It calmed me as I waited for Mac, for what seemed an eternity even if it was only minutes. Somehow, someway, I knew we would all be on that plane. The agent spotted him before I did, his head bobbing up and down well above the other passengers making their ways, belt and shoes in hand, racing down the hall. She called into the crew to tell them to hold the doors. I was so relieved, even if not happy, and I thanked heaven as we headed high into the morning sky.

What goes up, must come down though. It was, as imagined, a brutally painful afternoon. One made even more so when I would get not five minutes of privacy with my dying mom to say our goodbye before my older sister chose to come back into the room. I chose to stay silent so my last few moments with my mother were as peaceful as possible for her, remembering her upset and overwhelm in the hospital as my older and younger sister argued over her release. The next night as Susie retreated to my parents' guest bedroom, I fell asleep in my mom's bed, head on her Clinique scented pillow, before we flew back to New York the next day, March 15. I'm awakened around 4:30 a.m. by an alert on my phone. And even though there was no text to accompany the ding, I decided to stay awake, knowing I only had a few hours left before we would be leaving for the airport, choosing to use that precious time to finish the conversation that had been cut short at the hospice.

I felt my mom's presence so strongly as I propped up the pillows to sit and speak with her. It was a special few moments that ended with me deciding to text her; it seemed like the most right and perfect way to end our "conversation." She was in and out of consciousness, mostly out by then and I knew she wouldn't see it, but I wanted to honor that time with her in some tangible way. I sent a GIF I had recently come upon—it was a beautiful beating heart, moving through a rainbow of colors as it pulsed. I couldn't transport my whole physical body through time and space to be physically with her at that moment but I knew my heart moved through those wavelengths and touched hers in that very second I hit send. She passed over late the next night,

March 16. Susie was born on March 17, a Saint Patrick's Day baby. My dad had died the day before my brother's birthday. I somehow knew the sixteenth would be the day my mom would choose, knowing she would never want to leave on her child's birthday.

The morning of the sixteenth, my mind moved momentarily to my recently deceased dog Scrappy, having died just four months before—his death had devastated me. My mom sent me a YouTube video with a song by Kenny Rogers I'd never seen or heard, "Goodbye." As I listened, I sobbed, but my doorbell ringing broke my bawl. A beautiful *coincidence*, right there midsong, Scrappy's ashes had arrived home.

Not many days later I sent a text to a friend who had just recently gotten a new pup. I'd sent some treats of Scrappy's that'd yet to be opened before he fell ill and she had reached out to thank me, including pictures. Just after hitting send on my text back to Jane, I opened my Daily Guidepost to be greeted by John 16:22: "So with you: Now is your time of grief, but I will see you again and you will rejoice, and no one will take away your joy." It brought me much comfort that morning, deep in grief over Scrappy's death.

Fast forward a few months to the morning of March 16 when I was comforted again when that same John verse began that day's Guidepost. And on this special day, Sabra, who had written that impactful Guidepost message after Scrappy's death, *coincidentally* was again the author, this time sharing an even more consoling story about death and those who watch over us from heaven, sharing about her mother hanging lights on their porch after Sabra's sister had died, wanting her daughter to be able to spot the house from heaven. And what soothing synchronicity that was—just the day before, in the last few moments at my mom's before heading back to New York, I spotted an unopened box of decorative lights in her kitchen drawer and decided to take them to hang on my bungalow porch. It couldn't have been a more special entry to start the day my mother would die.

*   *   *

As I prepare to return to New York after a Florida memorial had been arranged by some of my siblings, knowing I'd probably never again step foot in my parents' home with all that was going on within our family, I decide to take a piece of her luggage to accompany my carry-on, a purple wheely bag catching my attention in her closet.

On those first few trips for my dad's passing anniversary, we had a bit of a routine for those few days we had together, an important one being going to the beach with his ashes where we were slowly letting go of him and sprinkling some each year in the Gulf of Mexico at the precise moment he passed. Those first years after he died were incredibly beautiful ones for me and my mom as we started to bridge our own gap to friendship. She was opening up a bit more, sharing a little more about her own past, her own present, and her own hopes for her future on that beach. After we'd spread the ashes, we would lunch at Sharky's on the water. Then onto Publix and Target and Bells, where we would laugh a lot, traversing the aisles with our carts and Starbucks. And there was always a reorganizing of her walk-in closet, which got even more hysterical as I would ask her how in the world she'd decided on some certain pieces.

"It was on sale," she'd always respond.

She could never resist a mega-markdown, even if she might never-ever even wear it! But so many sales, so much time spent making her way around store aisles, had overstuffed her closet. It was always a disorganized disaster of a mess, and I'd spend hours in there, her, right outside on the bed, with us chatting and chuckling, as I color coded the pieces by style and restored order to the shambles. We'd double over some of those nights in laughter. Well, I'd double over, while my mom would cross her legs to stop from peeing in her pants and wetting the bed. The chatter would turn deeper . . . well, as deep as it could get for her, at least as far as her expressions. Her mind and her inside, I feel strongly, dove deeper about lots of things yet, communicating her opinions, where she stood on issues, sharing her insights, her thoughts, and feelings, and emotions were rarely shared on her outside.

I was newly separated after my long struggle to end the marriage and in the process of that status changing to divorce during those few pivotal visits with my mom. I was also newly in love. Those moments of bonding came about as I shared myself with her in ways I'd never felt able or comfortable to do before. Those memories are precious to me. Her words and responses to all I was sharing about my own life gifted me much support and understanding, along with the very little she shared from her own inside, confirmed much I'd long suspected about her relationship with my dad. These visits together also gave me holy insight into her heart, her own hope, her own truth about true love.

As I walk through her closet on that morning after her memorial, with my hand running along and touching all her clothes, many of those sale items still having their tags on them, I spot the bag tucked away in the corner. Upon opening, I see a piece of paper. It was a print out from Priceline.com with her itinerary from her trip to Las Vegas in July 2012. I smiled at first, at the memory of my mom, the hoarder, having kept that for eleven years! The chuckle changed quickly though, as tears streamed down my cheeks. I met up with her there on that trip. It was the anniversary weekend *he* had set for our reunion. She was set to meet an old special friend of hers there as well. What a gift it was for me that morning, to be reminded she will travel with me now, just as she was with me then, on another heart wrenching morning many years earlier in Las Vegas.

* * *

It's April and the city has come alive in its springtime glory while I attentively finish writing my mom's eulogy only hours before her New York City service is set to begin. I read it to my mom and dad as I sit in the dark of my bedroom, then lay my head down for a short rest before making my way to the church. Josh Groban and Sara Bareilles sing me to sleep with "Both Sides Now" after I ask my parents what they think of my eulogy. My Pandora shuffle brings them into bed to comfort me and I feel certain both have given me their blessing.

I'm afraid of going over the time limit the priest asked us each to stick to, so when my turn comes to share my heart, I read through the pages quicker than I wanted to, but other than that, I feel at peace with what and how I honored the gentle and caring newborn-baby nurse who I was blessed to call my mother; especially the last few sentences:

Thank you, Mom. For Dad's, yes, but also YOUR help to choose a journey for my own self, even if I'm still learning how to truly soar on that journey. Trusting in your gentle hands to help me navigate, faithful there is a strong, supportive grip holding mine, swaddled in your everlasting love, sure as sure could ever be in its unconditional and constant presence in my life, keeps me breathing easier, knowing your wings now, along with your hands, your beautiful heart and exquisite successes fly with me, while they light my way at the same time.

And so beautiful to me to make the connection that when my dad died, his funeral, taking place at the same church, his luncheon after at the same restaurant, was April 16, a day after we would hold my mom's fourteen years later on April 15. A full circle wink and nod to remind me and help me to return to trust; that everything is happening right and perfectly even if, and when, it feels very much the opposite. There is always help with a much bigger picture our minds can't always make sense of but our souls are always in sync with and connected to via a very beautiful spiral stairway to heaven. And when body, mind, and soul are aligned—what beautiful possibilities for all our stories.

But even in that holy, sacred beauty, April is stomping me. My birthday week is especially brutal. I stare at the prayer card we had made for her memorial longer each day, as we inch closer to my birthday. I'm begging the Hindu Wheel of Life on the one side of that card to work its magic on me again as I am about to start another trip around the sun.

The end of the month offers a brief respite in the strangest of ways as I somehow stumble upon an updated remake of the original film *The Little Prince* while scrolling online for a movie to help me decompress. I'd not heard about it, even though it had been released in the US in the summer of 2016. At that time, as shock and distress continued to mount following my first book's release, simultaneously, there was sibling dysfunction that was escalating exponentially, and tensions with my ex continuing to barrel backward. I missed it, not surprisingly. After watching it, a beautiful moment of synchronicity became crystal and clear to me . . . the movie was meant to wait until that exact now precious moment in time to view it. The inclusion of the poignant side story about a mother and her daughter to update the classic tale that holds so much meaning for me personally since I'd played the part as a young girl, turned my mood for those two blessed hours. I laughed and cried my way through it. My mom was a hoarder herself just like Jeff Bridge's pilot and I have no doubt it was a birthday gift from her to help me smile, and let me know she was with me. As I watched the relationship that modernizes some of the themes of the original story morph and grow, another special present, the realization she was supporting me in ways she was never able to in her human life, now, comes to me and brings great comfort. My mother's life and choices were her own, even though she probably felt many decisions were not options or possibilities. And while she and I chose different paths for a similar road we both walked, her support to me after I faced my own crossroad in the most important relationship we can have with another person, our most intimate significant other, didn't just encourage me, it created a bond that remains a priceless treasure to me. Even though the bond became severely stressed after barely beginning a beautiful new relationship in those few years just after my dad died, it didn't break. And I not only have hung onto that precious gossamer of a thread, it has been nurtured and strengthened in the time since she passed over. I'd been asked in an interview after *EaaHE* won the 2016 N. N. Light Best Non-Fiction Award if I could have a superpower, and I answered—invisibility, so to help shed light on all the unknowns that took over my life. A wink and a nod and a bit of an ironic twist to *want* to be invisible after years of feeling invisible. And a very divine assist from my mother after she passed over, knowing exactly how that felt when she herself was alive.

When I reflect on our relationship, and I won't speak for her, I can only share for myself that one of her greatest gifts to me was the help she gave during those few precious visits together, and continues to give me, to stay true to myself. That truth I strayed from after taking the journey of my life to finally fully embrace it was possible to be returned to only because she has held my hand so lovingly from heaven. That fragile time just a few weeks after she died, trying to celebrate my own life while yet struggling with grief so intensely, she reminded me of both our own shared stuff, even though we each may have dealt with much of it differently as I watched that very different mom and daughter transform their relationship. You don't have to be in a relationship with a beater or a cheater, or any partner that society traditionally deems unworthy of staying in, to end it. Leaving, because you are not "in love" *is* enough. Whether you and your partner were in love and are unable to return to that place via therapy and counseling combined with a commitment of the two in the relationship to repair, mend, and rebuild the relationship after it was lost or broken, or you have made your way to a place of acceptance that which was never there cannot be recreated, rekindled, or rebuilt . . . your unhappiness and dissatisfaction in the relationship is worthy enough a reason to end things. *You* are important enough to live a joyful life. It is God's greatest gift to us to freely choose. It's never too late to take that belief and trust into your heart and claim that truth for yourself. And it is never too late to return to it, reclaim it if we've forgotten it . . . gift yourself with your All-In for you and the tools you need to stay true to yourself and your All-In.

When I reflect, I realize that many of my most powerful lessons I have relearned and reawakened to have been through my main tool— running. While participating in the More Magazine half marathon one year, I read the back of another's shirt. She became a pacer for me, following right behind. It can be easy to lose track of time as the miles start to rack up and your body starts to slow down. I read its words over and again as I rounded the Central Park pavement behind her. I loved it so much I found a site where you could create your own clothes, and I made one for myself, for my running buddy Jane, and a few friends I felt would love it as much as me: "The woman who starts the race isn't the same one who finishes the race." What a reminder as I ran that day: The gift of patience and fortitude I had finally given to myself had made a huge difference in my ability to make some different choices for myself, the most important being the change in the relationship I had with my then-husband. When I finally started to be gentler with myself and take the time to just breathe through some certain difficult times instead of feeling a failure because I had allowed them in the first place, it was then that everything started to change for me. Berating myself had never worked well, and the flip to being kinder was what helped me baby step through a complete and total transformation, with a few faithful fantastical leaps at the right and perfect time to balance them. But, for the most part I moved slowly, and thoughtfully. Instead of losing patience and scolding myself for all the things we can usually find to berate and betray our own selves, I decided to keep the faith, and treat myself with a little more tenderness. Whether it's a new weight, a new job, a new relationship, or a whole new life one is wanting for themselves, it can be daunting and overwhelming and certainly discouraging when only focused on the end result. Holding your mind's eye's visions are so important, yet, holding your form the best you can through each and every day is what moves you to that vision and often, just zeroing in on the babysteps necessary to make it through one beautiful but brutally challenging day is the most important thing we can do for ourselves.

I agree with a quote by Hemingway that made its way to me as I've written, and written, these last few years, "There is nothing to writing. All you have to do is sit down at a typewriter and bleed." For a while I was afraid I just might bleed out, but, as I held my form through it, hour by hour, the opposite happened as it began to fill me back up. The tide did eventually begin to turn. I did eventually come full circle. Again.

My father helped me believe it before, my mom helps me remember it now: It's never too late. I can forget, and remember, and circle around as many times as it takes . . . but I can do it. Whatever *it* is, I can make my way through.

* * *

The summer that followed my reconnection with *him*, just after my dad died, I reached out to him late one night, so elated I literally leapt from my seat after winning my first official hand of poker. I had decided to play in our community's annual Labor Day poker tourney. My dad had probably played in dozens of them when he was alive and I wanted to honor him by taking a seat at the table myself. *He* tutored me for a few days before I sat down at the table since I'd never played before. It was his advice if I found myself in a situation in which I was unsure how to proceed to take my chances and just go All-In that resulted in me jumping up and down in delight upon winning the very first hand of the game. My cousin had challenged me, bullied me, but I called his bluff, gambled all my chips . . . and won the hand. I couldn't wait to share it. There was no way I could not, *not* reach to *him*.

Ten years later I not only wasn't able to jump up and down about much anymore, but it was painful to even put my feet to the floor many mornings. Who knew, a journey to heal my mind would not only renew my trust and faith in the divine Universe, but deepen it. I thank God, my father, and a whole army of angels and guides and friends, for helping me remember something very important—I want to live. I want to love. I want to make love. I want to jump for joy. I want to feel at peace. After a lifetime afraid to risk anything, let alone everything for love, a holy sacred circle to be gifted to round once, but to full circle in faith again, an even more beautiful present.

Just like the bracelet I gave *him* years back, bought before we reconnected, before Larry and I even separated, not having any idea who it was for at the time I purchased it, only that it spoke to me so strongly when I came upon it. I'd spent the day in quiet contemplation along the waters in a neighboring Jersey shore town not too far from my bungalow as my heart raced and beat off balance after a cortisone injection did not sit well with the shape my heart was in at that time, struggling mightily with my want and desire to end the marriage but unable to take the actual physical steps to do so. It was more money than I felt I *should* spend on a piece of jewelry I had no recipient for, and I didn't buy it that day, but it kept returning to my mind. And heart. After a wink and a nod from God placed it before me not long after in NYC more than once within a couple weeks, I would wind up ordering it and tucking it away in a special place for a special time for a special someone I might never even meet. But I bought it anyway. Something whispered to me, and I listened. The strong silver cuff had a quote on it from Rainer Maria Rilke's *Letters to a Young Poet*: "Don't search for the answers, which could not be given to you now, because you would not be able to live them. And the point is to live everything. Live the questions now. Perhaps, then, someday far into the future, you will gradually, without even noticing it, live your way into the answer."

I've thought of that bracelet often since buying it for an unknown someone, someday, maybe, after my own struggle of living my way in search of some important answers to some holy, sacred questions. It is front and center in my heart as I devote myself to making my way there again. Just like Sarah had to do in the TV show *Parenthood*, as she found herself searching through those seasons of her reel life that led her to a hospital parking lot where her true love told her he wanted to go All-In too. I keep faith it all makes *sense* on the other side, but here in humanity interpreting the reasons for our most important relationships, understanding what these pivotal relationships mean and why things are happening the way they are can be so difficult, even if the connections can be so clearly recognized. Then, *accepting* them for what they truly are, and what that means for our very real lives . . . the journey of a lifetime sometimes. Sometimes, two.

Somehow, Someway

Her one year anniversary is almost upon me. She is on my mind almost constantly. I'm grateful to have the awareness of her death day's approach, and not just because my baby sister and I are dealing with lawyers and siblings we would both rather not. My mom is everywhere, quite simply, because I want her with me. It was raining one morning when a cardinal landed on my terrace as I was sitting quietly, sipping my cappuccino after tossing out breakfast for the birds and squirrels, listening to the water bouncing off the wrought iron bistro set that sits on it.

I love the rain. The sound, music to my ears as the melody of the skies mixes with the lyrics of the earth. It is heavenly indeed to me. The bright red bird walked right up to the glass door, and, against a grey backdrop of the day, stayed for a few seconds, staring right at me, before making a turn and flying back off into the raindrops. Red was my mom's favorite color. Feeling held by the hope of true love, on this somber but sacred March morning, she just reminded me . . . she isn't just alive in my memory . . . she's really, truly with me.

Her death had sent me reeling this past year. Even though I'd felt sure I had made peace with our relationship, and the choices I had made, the time after her death pummeled me. That day in her hospice room, before my older sister cut my private time with her short, I cried as I told her I was sorry, so sure she would get to hear the truth from the one person who could *fix* all of this. Even though high as a kite on morphine by that point, she was able to ground herself enough to take tighter hold of my hand as she assured me, "Tia, I promise you, I already know the truth." Even though her words meant the world to me, and I believe her wholeheartedly, I struggled after, feeling I'd let her down, as I'd felt many times as a young girl. It was similar to the disappointment I had felt I was as I struggled after my dad died, convincing myself that I'd let him down by being grounded at the Atlanta airport instead of standing by his bedside before he lost consciousness.

But, where I'd been able to move through my mourning much differently after my dad's death, even in my grief and the guilt I put on my own shoulders that I hadn't made it to my best friend's side before he slipped into an unconscious state, it was a year after my mom's passing and I was still struggling mightily. Almost more at this point than at the immediate aftermath of her death. Why I continued to hold my grief so close over the passing year instead of releasing it was because during that period of my most-exquisite-roller-coaster love story, I had chosen *him* over her. And while I have no regrets, it doesn't mean that, now after all these years of stepping forward and backward and forward on my cyclical healing journey, it wasn't a painful choice to make, and one I will always wish never had had to be made.

As my heart aches with this knowledge, I utilize my spiritual tools and a session with Monique, as it always does, soothes my sorrowful, wearied heart. "Tia, this story is beautiful. You must believe that. You must trust that. YOU are beautiful. All on your own."

She reminds me that love is an energy and science assures us energy can never be destroyed. She comforts me as she reminds me that the bond my mom and I created, no matter how late, even if we chose not to nurture it the same way me and my dad chose to ours, remains firmly in place. As scary as Monique's all-on-your-own message is, the most peaceful wave of calm washes over me at the same time. In that magnificent moment, I'm able to embrace the beauty of *this* story. The one God and I know is real, true, and beautiful. My mom knows it too. And even though I don't know how long this moment will last before I have to reach out and grab hold of it again after it may slip from my fingers, I will cling to it *now*, and be grateful for it. In that sense of stillness, after traveling around another circle to find myself again, fall in love with my own self again, I know that somehow, someway—especially now that I can kneel again, even if I still can't full circle my bicycle pedals yet—I can always stop, drop, and pray a prayer of thanks that I keep making it back there again. To myself. To my All-In.

Epilogue: Somewhere Over the Rainbow

We don't prove our divinity by denying our humanity.
—Unknown

T hose Little Feat lyrics I listened to in one of the most beautiful love letters ever given to me ... who knew how special they were to my story when the gods above, in full view of a big picture and a very divine blueprint, helped me to trust, and take them to heart. Our happy endings depend on it—whether poetry on pages, words in chapters, or as we sing the very real songs of our lives. To be "Willin'," not just wanting. Intending, not just desiring. Dreaming, not just living. Living, not just dreaming. And praying. Definitely still praying.

I'm All-In for all that.

I began book one with Carl Jung fostering a belief for me, "The unexpected and the incredible belong in this world. Only then is life whole." It seems right and perfect to close this second book on his words as well. "You have the potential to become the best version of yourself; use this gift with constant gratitude. Every day is the ability to discover, explore, and practice on the mission to find your purpose. Remember that your greatest life achievements derive from being your authentic self."

And, now that I can kneel again, even if I still can't full circle my bicycle pedals yet, I stop, drop, and pray a prayer of thanks that I made it back there again. To myself.

And I'll full circle back to one last quote, one I included in my first book but somehow wound up with an "unknown" credit at that time and feels right and perfect for this second . . .

When we surrender, we allow the Universe to work its magic; we say yes to infinite possibilities; we trust that things will work out as they are meant to; and we give ourselves permission to let go of the outcome. This can be liberating, intimidating, blissful, scary, and a swirl of so many other emotions. But, in the end, if we are true to our heart, life unfolds with magnificence, and we get to celebrate.

—davidji

Favorites

Abraham-Hicks.com

Esther, Abraham, and Jerry too always remind me of the "beauty full" advice my father gave me often in his last few years, *"If it were me . . ."*

SpiritualMediaBlog.com

Matthew was one of the few who returned my email about *Everything and a Happy Ending*. His reply came the day of my dad's golf tournament. A wink and a nod no doubt.

Kevin Stock's *Yourdrum*

A lovely reminder to me about the magic we allow when we beat to our own drum.

Kim Krans Archetypes Tarot Deck

I was afraid of it at first. I faced it. I fell in love with it. I let it transform me.

LorieLadd.com

She's taken me on a journey with the Orions, we've meditated with the Andromedans, and she reconnected me with the Pleiadeans. I'm grateful for so many new friends.

Ashwagandha, Gaba, L-theanine, & Ryze Mushroom coffee

An ancient medicinal herb, amino acids & therapeutic, natural, *magical* mushrooms that all assist my body, mind, and soul for so many calming reasons.

Sesame seed oil nasal washes

Sesame oil is not just an antibacterial but anti-inflammatory, antiviral, and antifungal. A few drops of sesame oil and a couple shakes of sea salt helped me breathe easier through the coronavirus.

Bi(o)lateral music

Similar to the way the binaural beats the Holosync meditation system Centrepointe assisted with, the "beauty full" music helps soothe my brain.

A Beautiful Day in the Neighborhood

Fate would sit me to watch this beauty full movie on the last day of February in a leap year. A right and perfect time to take another.

When Lloyd's dad shares with him that he feels *he finally understands how to live as he faces death*, I heard my own father whisper to me.

I love you too, Dad.

Yeonmi Park's *In Order to Live*
She became a favorite in two faithful sentences ...

"I learned something else that day: We all have our deserts. They may not be the same as my desert, but we all have to cross them to find a purpose in life and be free."

Lastly, which remains most important to me, my Doc Johnson Pocket Rocket—still my favorite of the group.

Acknowledgments

Michael Ignatieff has said, "One of the greatest feelings in life is the conviction you've lived the life you wanted to; with the rough and the smooth, the good and the bad—but yours, shaped by your own choices, not someone else's."

To all those who helped on the adventure I set out on to live the life I want; with the rough and the smooth, the good and the bad, shaped by my own choices, thank you. I'm grateful to each and every one of you, but most especially . . .

Neale Donald Walsch: I believe God wants you to know . . . I'm so very grateful for you. *Your friend, Tia*

Monique: MoniqueArcand.com
Your assistance through some of those moments that can change everything in a heartbeat helped save not just my story but my life.

"Tia, take a deep breath—transcend your state of mind even for a moment."

Susie: My realest friend. My truest family.

Stephen John Shurina II: You gave me life, a second chance at it, then helped save it. A trifecta of a lifetime.
Your song is in my soul.
—Dan Fogelberg, *"Leader of the Band"*

Oprah and Deepak: The 2020 meditation series moved me through a virus and wound up healing some of my most visceral wounds. 2021's continues to walk with me.
Ma Vid Visha Vahai—may harmony prevail.
What will you do with the light that is yours?

Jessica Buchanan & Ilsa Manning: I believe with all my heart it was my mom's hand on my shoulder that guided me to Soul Speak Press just after the one year anniversary of her death, knowing you were both the right and best hearts, and minds (& minds' eyes too) for my story.

To all the hashtags, accounts, friends, family, and foes who followed and unfollowed, communicated directly, indirectly, or silently, participated knowingly or not, helped actively in awareness with deliberate intention or not.

Some really moved me. All truly touched me. Each and every one a divine reminder and return for me.

A chance—a choice—to rise above the fear for me.

You gain strength, courage, and confidence
by every experience in which you really stop to look fear in the face . . .
do the thing you think you cannot do.
—Eleanor Roosevelt

www.ingramcontent.com/pod-product-compliance
Lightning Source LLC
Chambersburg PA
CBHW031527120626
46545CB00005B/2038